PHILIP AUGUSTUS

PHILIP AUGUSTUS

BY

WILLIAM HOLDEN HUTTON, B.D.

KENNIKAT PRESS
Port Washington, N. Y./London

PHILIP AUGUSTUS

First published in 1896
Reissued in 1970 by Kennikat Press
Library of Congress Catalog Card No: 75-112809
ISBN 0-8046-1076-2

Manufactured by Taylor Publishing Company   Dallas, Texas

CONTENTS

CHAPTER I

FRANCE at the beginning of the twelfth century was one of the smallest and least important of the European states. The duchy of France—a title borne for three centuries by the house of Robert the Strong—was no domain exactly bounded and compact. Its lands were situated not only in the country between the Seine and the Loire, but lay in small and scattered fragments farther south, in Poitou, and in the north. Peculiar rights belonged to the king in distant towns and churches. He was lord in Orleans. He was abbat of S. Martin's at Tours and senior canon of the church of S. Quentin. And step by step within the lands of the great lords of the north, of the great dukes and the great ecclesiastics, he acquired new rights, by intervening to check some injustice or win some privilege on behalf of a lesser lord.

The royal domain was the strength of the early Capets. As rich lords they could stand against the barons who hedged them in, and appear, unlike the Karlings, at least the equals of their great vassals. But the territory which they possessed was small,

and their material resources, in comparison with those
of other European states, were contemptible. Entering
rarely into foreign politics, and then with a conspicuous
absence of dignity or success, the royal house of France
saw its kingdom surrounded by foes or lukewarm
friends, nearly every one of whom was superior to itself
in strength. To the north and east the Empire and
Lorraine, the great dynasties of Flanders and Burgundy,
were each more than an equal combatant for the Frankish king. Southwards the kingdom of Arles, sometimes
close linked to the Empire, sometimes enjoying a precarious independence, stood aloof, with many marches
and counties, from the influence of the central realm.
The great dukes of Aquitaine and the proud house that
ruled in Toulouse scarce in their most friendly moments
professed any allegiance to the Capets. And the demon
race, sprung, said legends, from the union of an Angevin
count with an unearthly bride, which ruled on the banks
of the lower Loire and the Maine, the borderland
between France, Aquitaine, and Brittany, was gathering
its powers in grim concentration of purpose for a wider
sweep, which should endanger the throne of the Frankish
king. The circle was completed by the great duchy of
Normandy, to which was annexed the county of Maine.

But small as was· its territory and slight its power,
the house which ruled from Paris claimed all the prerogatives and dignity of the imperial line which it had
dispossessed. It clung with sagacious tenacity to the
assertion that it was the successor of the line of Charles
the Great. Hugh Capet had been elected in 987 by the
influence of the Church at a moment when the Karling
race had dwindled into impotent decadence. He had him-

self been a great feudal lord, the greatest and strongest of
his peers. He had large possessions, his brother Henry
held Burgundy for him, the dukes of Normandy and
Aquitaine were his brothers - in - law, the count of
Vermandois was of his kin. In the twelfth century his
descendants had lost the strength of his position. The
great duchies around them were in alien and often
hostile hands. But the grandeur of their theoretical
claim was not abandoned. They were still far above
the feudal hierarchy, as the heirs of the Cæsars, sovereigns
by divine right, the lawful kings of the West Franks.

The monarchy of the twelfth century was absolute
in principle. It claimed to be the source of all power
and authority, to hold in its own hand the control of all
local and central government. More than this, it was
founded on an alliance with the Church, which, in spite
of their persistent moral lapses, the kings had shown the
keenest anxiety to keep intact. It had seemed at one
time as if the irresistible movement of the feudal
theory, which had transmuted all offices into fiefs,
and swept all ancient survivals into the net of its
universal encroachment, would overwhelm the monarchy as it had transformed the nobility and invaded
the Church. And indeed in his relations with those who
held land directly under him the Capetian king had
fallen under the domination of the feudal claim. He was
a lord like other lords, with vassals whose dues were
limited and whose rights were secured. But he never
ceased to be sovereign as well as suzerain, and the persistence of his assertion of the old monarchical theory,
even in the period of his greatest weakness, preserved
the idea and prepared the way of the absolute monarchy

that was to rise in the thirteenth century above the mighty vassals which had surrounded its territories and limited its powers.

The monarchy of the Capets then was never a feudal monarchy, however closely it might be embedded in feudalism.   The king was a real king, not a mere *primus inter pares*.   The exercise of his power and the geographical limits of its extension might be restricted, but he still acted as sovereign where he could, and waited for the time when all the authority of his predecessors should be exerted without restraint.   The sovereign who raised the French monarchy to the height which its most sanguine supporters in the tenth century had scarce dared to predict for it was Philip Augustus, who shares with two very different men—S. Louis and Louis XI.—the fame of having created the power which became the arbiter of Europe. But his work, great as it was, was built on foundations which others had laid.   It is impossible to understand his reign without a sketch of those of his father and grandfather.

Louis VI., who came to the throne as sole king in 1108, had already proved his prowess by his suppression of the barbarities and disorders of the barons of the domain.   He identified the interests of the crown with the assertion of the principles of good government. Engaged throughout his reign in perpetual wars, he yet managed, by diplomacy as well as military skill, to raise the monarchy far above the position which any of his house had achieved.   Centralisation was his chief aim,—and the concentration of his power within the royal domain.   He ceased to make journeys through

the distant fiefs.   Towards them his attitude was almost
always hostile.   He set himself, by stern repression of
disorder, by constant espousal of the interests of the
Church and the rising towns, to become master of his
own domain and to base his sway upon his protection
and his justice.   Like an eager landlord adding field
to field, he was constantly increasing the royal domain
by purchase, confiscation, and escheat.   And what he
acquired he brought to order and submission.   Year
by year he went about redressing the wrongs of churches
and monasteries, and reducing the barons—a Hugh du
Puiset, a Thomas de Marle, men infamous for their
devastations and their vices—to subservient peace.   Year
by year he visited town after town, heard cases, issued
establishments, which gave the monarchy new roots in
the affection of the people.   Against Henry I. of England
he was as persistent a foe as his external weakness
would allow.   Often compelled to give way and tem-
porise, he yet really held his own, and the marriage
which united the Angevin lands to the fiefs of the
Norman house in 1128 seemed to be more than counter-
balanced by the wedding in 1137 of the heir of France
with the heiress of Aquitaine.

Almost at the moment of his son's marriage Louis
VI. died.   He had done much to make his small state
firm and compact.   By his last diplomatic triumph he
seemed to have opened a new era of extension for the
monarchy.   France and Aquitaine under one rule
should be ever striving to unite ; and the house of
Anjou, whose hasty and reckless Count Geoffrey Court-
mantel had to fight for his wife's lands as well as his
own, might well by a strong attack from north and south

have been swept away. But the great opportunities needed a statesman and a warrior to use them. "La France attendait un grand homme," says Martin, "mais le grand homme ne parut pas."

The earlier part of the reign of Louis VII., while the great Suger, the friend and minister of his father, still watched over his career, was not without strength and vigour. He held his own against pope and barons. He watched the struggle of Geoffrey of Anjou for Normandy with a sagacious abstention from active intervention, and received as reward the castle of Gisors. But the period of prosperity was ended by the call to a crusade. The voice of S. Bernard called kings and peoples to succour the Christians of the East, and Louis VII. sacrificed the prosperity of his country and the strength of his rule to what seemed a still more urgent and imperative demand. The wise rule of Suger, 1147-1150, could do no more, with all its vigour, than avert disaster during the king's absence.

On his return Louis found himself confronted by new difficulties. The most serious of them was of his own making. On March 18, 1152, an ecclesiastical council at Beaugency, near Orleans, pronounced the nullity of his marriage with Eleanor of Aquitaine. The cause which was considered sufficient was the fact that Hugh Capet, from whom Louis VII. was fifth in descent, had married a sister of the great-great-grandfather of Eleanor. When this was recognised as a sufficient cause, we can scarcely wonder that Philip Augustus should have anticipated no difficulty in freeing himself from his wife Ingeborgis. Closer personal reasons were the opinion which Louis had formed of his wife's character and the contempt

which she did not hesitate to express for his pious and
simple life.   Strong as may have been the personal causes
for the dissolution of the alliance, no greater political
blunder could have been committed.   The duchy of
Aquitaine, with the county of Poitou—a district stretch-
ing from the Creuse to the Adour, and from Lyons to the
Bay of Biscay—had hardly begun to feel it possible that
it should be permanently united to the French monarchy
when it was again severed.   Two months later it was
united to the power which most threatened the growth
of the French kingdom.   Eleanor, sought of many
interested suitors, became, on May 18, 1152, the wife of
a boy fourteen years her junior—Henry, the young
count of Anjou, the heir to the great possessions of the
Norman house from which his mother sprang.   A few
months more, and before the year 1154 was ended, Louis
VII. found himself confronted by a young and vigorous
rival, the husband of his former wife, who was king of
the English, overlord of Scotland and Wales, duke of
Normandy and Aquitaine, count of Poitou, Anjou,
Maine, and Touraine.   He was opposed at his own
doors by what might claim to be called a great continental empire.

Within the next few years causes of disagreement
sprang up on every side.   Henry laid claim to the
homage of Toulouse, laid hands on Auvergne, pressed
his encroachments into Berry, formed a strong alliance
with Flanders, and by the marriage of his third son
acquired control of Brittany.   Louis attempted to resist
the pressure of this dangerous environment by a policy
of quiescence aided by secret diplomacy ; and, on the
whole, he succeeded.   He took for second wife Con-

stance, daughter of Alfonso, king of Castile and Leon.
He gave his sister in marriage to Raymond V., count
of Toulouse.   Thus he did something to counteract
the Angevin influence in the south.   He made a marriage treaty with his great rival, by which his little
daughter Margaret and Henry's eldest boy were betrothed.   On his wife's death in 1160 he married Alice
of Champagne, daughter of Count Thibault V., whose
four brothers, William, an ecclesiastic; Henry, count of
Champagne and Brie; Thibault, count of Chartres and
Blois; and Stephen, count of Sancerre, formed the
strongest family alliance that could be opposed to the
menacing power of Henry II.   He maintained a firm
alliance with the orthodox pope, Alexander III.   He
showed himself a constant vindicator of ecclesiastical
rights.   When his rival's minister, Thomas Becket, the
greatest prelate of the age, fled from his dominions,
Louis gave him refuge in his own lands, and steadily,
in spite of the strongest pressure, maintained his cause
against the jealous anger of the English king.   Sputters
of war broke from time to time across the sky, but
Louis, if not strong enough to resist for long, lost little
by any of the disturbances.   Again and again, half
secretly, half openly, he stirred up and supported the
rebellious sons against their father, notably in the great
and dangerous insurrection of 1173.

By every means Louis strove to extend his influence
outside the royal domain, which his father had rendered
strong and submissive.   With the great ecclesiastics he
was in constant and amicable relations.   With the rising
liberties of the towns he showed himself to be in
sympathy by many grants of privilege and charters of

incorporation.   Outside his domain he appeared in arms
in the valley of the Rhone, in Auvergne, and in Velay.
In Languedoc he was in constant communication with
the barons who chafed under the Angevin rule.   Bertrand
de Born, most gallant of knights and of troubadours,
called to him loudly to vindicate the rights of his crown.
He was content not to answer the appeal, but to neglect
no means of confirming his southern alliances.   It was
a day of small things, and among small measures only
could the ruler of the French kingdom take his way.
From a military point of view the power of the crown
had fallen back, but diplomacy gave a different aspect
in which to view its position.

The later years of Louis VII. showed the power of
the crown gradually increasing, but still feeble indeed
in comparison with the great states by which it was
surrounded.   The Empire under Frederic I., one of
the greatest of medieval monarchs, had triumphed over
the Italian cities, and made a concordat with the pope,
by which the imperial power, if it had nominally retired
from some of its pretensions, was certainly not in reality
the weaker.   At a critical juncture it had seemed
probable that the emperor would even intervene in
French politics.   He remained a strong power on the
eastern frontier, and a source of support to the border
bishoprics and great lay fiefs in any quarrel that might
arise with the French king.   In the south too he held a
power which threatened that of the French crown.   In
1178 he was crowned king of Burgundy and Arles, and
thus entered into feudal relations with many fiefs over
which the French king claimed some authority.   But a
far more important factor in French politics was the

widespread and increasing power of the Angevin house
under the greatest of its rulers. The dominions of
Henry II. stretched from the Somme to the Pyrenees,
and included almost the whole of the land between the
Creuse and the Lot. Duke of Normandy, with the
practical command of Brittany ; duke of Aquitaine,
having imprisoned his wife, whose liberty might have
been dangerous as an encouragement to the intrigues of
the turbulent baronage of the south ; count of Anjou,
and Maine, and Touraine, lord of many petty counties
which impinged on the French kingdom at every point,
Henry II. confirmed, by diplomatic and military alliances,
the power which marriage and inheritance had founded.
The Lombard cities were his allies, his friends held the
passes of the Alps and the Pyrenees. Henry the Lion,
duke of Saxony, at one time the greatest territorial lord
in Europe, at another the banished possessor of but a
few northern cities, was his son-in-law. Alfonso IX.,
king of Castile, had married another of his daughters,
and was eager in seeking his counsel. With all the
Spanish kingdoms in turn he had relations, as with the
distant lands of Scandinavia, with Sicily, whose king was
his son-in-law, with Jerusalem, and the nearer powers of
Flanders and Burgundy. Year by year, by purchase
or exchange, by treaty or deliberate aggression, his
power over the small lordships which surrounded the
territory of the French king increased. Yet great as
was the external power of the English king, his position
was uneasy in the extreme. So long as his own extraordinary physical and mental vigour endured, he was
able to suppress his turbulent vassals, to overawe his
timid neighbours, and to conquer his rebellious sons.

But the extent of his possessions was too vast, the peoples submitted to his sway were too heterogeneous, for his power to endure after his death, or even to survive any cessation of his personal activity. In 1179 Henry's word was still thrice as powerful in Gaul as that of the king who reigned in Paris, but ten years later it would be seen that the whole current of affairs had set in a new direction.

Meanwhile the Frankish monarchy was advancing, less by a steady and deliberate policy than by fortunate accidents and a certain fitful sagacity of the monarch. The direct power of the crown extended over but a small part of Gaul, hardly more than the Ile-de-France, the Orléanais, and Picardy. But within that limited area the turbulence of the baronage had received severe checks. The châtelains, guardians of royal castles, whose position, originally official, had become a serious menace to the tranquillity of the country, to the peace of the church, and to the power of the crown, had, by the policy of Louis VI., continued by his successor, been almost extinguished. The smaller barons attended the royal summons with more alacrity, and the barons of the district round Paris, the lords of Beaumont and Montmorency, of Clermont and Dammartin, were learning to serve the crown as its more intimate servants and responsible officials. A gradual concentration of powers was preparing the monarchy to extend its influence. It was from within that the strength came before any serious attempt was made to use it outside. The great house of Champagne, holding also the county of Blois, hemmed in the royal domain in dangerous proximity. It was a diplomatic triumph to knit the princes of this powerful line in close alliance with the crown. In 1160, as has been said, Louis married Alice, daughter of the count of Blois and Champagne, whose elder brother was already seneschal, and whose second brother, William of the White Hands, was before long given the highest ecclesiastical dignity in the realm—the archbishopric of Rheims. The alliance was strengthened later by the marriage of one of Louis's daughters to Henry, count of Champagne, and of another to Thibault, count of Blois.

The extension of the royal influence thus obtained was increased by several definite steps, some of them proceeding from this alliance. In the north, through William of Rheims, Louis VII. won greatly increased authority. He entered into friendly relations with the bishops, and in some cases with the citizens, of Arras, Térouanne, Tournai, and Cambrai, while the bishoprics of Lorraine sought in him a protection from the encroachments of their duke. Himself, as men said, though not with complete truth, more of a monk than a king, Louis entered readily into friendly association with the great ecclesiastical fiefs which depended on the crown. In the duchy of Burgundy not only the great abbeys of Cluny and Tournus, but the bishoprics of Langres, Mâcon, Châlon, and Autun depended directly on the crown, and Louis did not allow the relation to be merely formal. In the political disputes of the Burgundian duchy he no less actively intervened. He encouraged the disagreements between the Duchess Mary and her son, Hugh III., and secured the submission of their dispute to the decision of his own court. He even intervened in the districts of the kingdom of Burgundy which depended feudally on the empire. His sister's son, Alberic of Toulouse, married the daughter of the dauphin of Vienne, from which, as Raymond V. wrote to the king, "there should be a gate opened for the increase of your realm, though this county of the dauphin belongs to the jurisdiction of the emperor." In the kingdom of Burgundy itself he found it impossible to withstand the power of Frederic, the emperor and king, but he succeeded in securing the election of his candidate to the archbishopric of Lyons, through whom he expected to receive no slight accession of political influence.

In central France Louis VII. never ceased to watch for occasions to protect the bishoprics and to grant them privileges for money. The material aid which he gave to the prelates in their struggles with neighbouring barons was more than returned by the moral support which he obtained from the Church. The ecclesiastical side of his policy, congenial to his own inclinations, was in reality no less conducive to the growth of his power. His most effective weapon against Henry II. was his continued support of Becket, which taught those who, for any reason, were discontented with the Angevin government to look for countenance to the king of the Franks.

In the south the great house of Toulouse retained much of its ancient power. Geographically, it was allied with Spain; historically, with the Empire. It has been observed that there is no historical record of a single performance from Toulouse of service at the king's court or in his host during the reign of the first five Capets. The counts of Toulouse in the twelfth century were

practically independent sovereigns. Louis's marriage
with Eleanor of Aquitaine gave him more direct relations with the southern districts, and though his divorce
severed his direct authority, his influence was not altogether obliterated. In 1154, by his second marriage
with Constance of Castile, he strengthened his association with the southern states, and he passed through
Languedoc on his way to Compostella—a progress which
was not without its political effects. By the marriage
of his sister Constance in the same year to Raymond V.
he acquired a more direct interest in the affairs of
Toulouse, and set up an opposition to the influence of
Henry II. in that region, whose claims, four years later,
he successfully withstood. With the southern sees he
approached an actual feudal connection. Over the barons
he began to assume some of the rights of a suzerain.
Before his death his name was at least well known
in Languedoc, and if his authority was not formally
recognised, the frequent appeals for his advice and
assistance had prepared the way for that recognition of
overlordship which the Albigensian war made inevitable.

It has been said by a great French historian that
the influence of Louis VII. was that of a moral conquest which prepared the way for the military successes
of his son. It may be added that his work, though not
striking or impressive, was genuine and durable. Philip
had little to inaugurate or to undo : he had chiefly to
continue and to accomplish.

CHAPTER II

THE BEGINNINGS OF PHILIP'S POWER

LOUIS'S first two marriages had given him no male heir. With his third wedding his hopes were renewed. On August 19, 1165, the expectations of the king and his people were gratified, and a boy was born.

There is some doubt as to where the heir so earnestly desired first saw the light. He is frequently by later writers called Philip of Gonesse, from a royal manor near Pontoise. In the great chronicle of Tours, the land of Gonesse is represented as his especial patrimony. Philip Mouskes, the historian of Tournai, shows that he was brought up there.

> A la Gonnesse fu nouris,
> S'ot non Felipes de Gonnesse.

But it is almost certain, from the contemporary poem of Peter Riga, that he was actually born at Paris; and Giraldus Cambrensis, who was studying in Paris at the time, gives a reminiscence which leaves little doubt on the point. In his delightful book, the *De Instructione Principum*, where he greatly glorifies the French kings at the expense of the English, he suddenly introduces a story of his own youthful experience. He says :—

"While in his early years, he who wrote this was at Paris, enthusiastically engaged in liberal studies, it chanced that one night at the very beginning of autumn, about the hour of the first sleep, shortly after the dead of night, it was said that by God's grace Philip had been born. This rumour was bruited through the city, and received with inexpressible delight. At once throughout the length and breadth of the city on every side there burst forth such a clamorous pealing of bells, and so great were the waxen lights kindled in every street, that those who knew not the cause of the unwonted tumult, the deafening sounds, and the universal illumination, imagined that some conflagration was even then threatening the city. The author of this work, who was at that time living in the city as a youth just completing his twentieth year, sprang from the bed on which he had but now fallen asleep, and hastened to the window. Looking out, he saw in the street two poor and miserable old crones carrying waxen candles before them; their countenances, their words, their gestures all alike expressed exultation as they hastened along with rapid steps, ever and anon meeting and jostling one another. He inquired of them what might be the cause of all this excitement and delight, whereupon one of them looked back and replied, 'Now we have a king given us by God, a mighty heir to the kingdom through God's bounty; through him shall fall on your king loss and disgrace, shame and heavy punishment, rich in confusion and distress.' Just as if she had openly said, 'A boy has been given us this night, who certainly by God's grace shall be the hammer of your king, and who also, beyond a doubt, shall

diminish the power and lands of him and his subjects.'
The woman knew that the author and his companions
were natives of England, and therefore it was that the
crone, as if in a spirit of prophecy, bitterly launched
forth against them and their king this sentence, which
was afterwards only too truly fulfilled."

It is a quaint picture of the dark narrow streets,
lighted on a sudden by the enthusiastic processions
which shouted the joyful news of the birth of the
"Godgiven" heir.   The young English scholar, aroused
from his sleep to listen to the boastful cries of the old
women, joined in the gratulations of the people.   From
every quarter messages of thankfulness reached the
king.   Even the city of Toulouse, far removed from
royal domination, proud in the freedom of its citizen
lords, "los baros de Tolosa," sent congratulations to the
French king.   A messenger brought the joyful news to
the abbey of S. Germain des Prés at the moment when
the monks sang "Blessed be the Lord God of Israel, for
He hath visited and redeemed His people."   Dieu-
donné, they cried out, is this new child of France—a
gift of God to king and people.

Scanty records reach us of the childhood of the "god-
given child."   He was brought up, as has been said, in
a county manor of the king.   He had a menagerie of
wild beasts to amuse him.   He was under the care of
learned clerks and statesmen.   Robert Clement, who
exercised much influence during the first year of his
reign, had watched over him for a long time.   He was
a bright and active child, eager to learn and quick at all
manly sports, a hunter from his youth.   Pious too he
was, said the clerkly chroniclers.   In the first year of his

reign his pure eyes saw the miracle of the mass in its reality. At S. Léger in Yveline, as the priest elevated the host, he saw a child of surpassing splendour, whom choirs of angels worshipped, and he adored with tears.

> Soli se regi detexit mystica virtus,
> Cui soli digne poterat res tanta patere.

As early as 1177 his father designed a marriage for him. He asked from Philip of Flanders the hand of his niece, the daughter of Matthew of Boulogne. But the project was abandoned.

A medieval king had generally but few years of schooling. His training in the work of government began early. It was so with Philip Augustus. He was not fourteen years old when, in the spring of 1179, his father was attacked by paralysis. Louis recovered, but, though only fifty-nine, he felt himself already an old man. He determined, after the fashion of his predecessors, to secure the succession by crowning his son in his lifetime. He had long postponed this customary ceremony. In spite of the urgent advice of the pope and the force of the custom of his fathers, he had declined even nominally to share his power with his young son. But illness, and the feeling that "his last days" were upon him, induced him to take steps at once for the election and coronation of Philip. Probably towards the end of April the archbishops, bishops, abbats, and barons met in the bishop's palace at Paris and heard the king's will that his son should be crowned. There is no reason to suppose that the formal election was omitted. All the prelates and barons, says Rigord, cried out "Fiat, fiat," and the king at once began the preparations for

the ceremony, which was to take place on the Feast of
the Assumption.   A proclamation was issued fixing the
day.

During the summer the king visited Compiègne, and
from thence the journey to Rheims for the coronation
was to be made.   The great forest, which still stretches
for miles to the south of the ancient city, was the
largest hunting-ground of the Frankish kings.   Here
the young Philip, now fourteen years old, went out
one day with companions to hunt.   They found a wild
boar, says Rigord's vivid story, and, uncoupling the
hounds, set chase after him with sounding horns through
the dark recesses of the woods.   Philip's horse bore
him more swiftly than his companions, till he had left
them far behind.   He found himself towards evening
quite alone, and in an absolutely secluded part of
the forest.   "Seeing himself left alone in that vast
solitude of wood, he began, not without reason, to be
afraid."   He looked anxiously from side to side, but saw
no signs of any human presence.   He crossed himself
devoutly and commended himself to God and the Blessed
Virgin and S. Denys, the patron and defender of the
kings of the Franks.   Hardly was his prayer over before
he saw a charcoal-burner, grim to behold, with face black
with charcoal, carrying a great axe on his shoulder.
The lad, when he saw him, feared somewhat, but,
recovering his courage, drew near and greeted him.
The man, when he knew to whom he was speaking,
left his work and brought him back to Compiègne.
The excitement and fatigue brought on a dangerous
illness, from which it seemed likely that the young
prince would not recover.   The king was in despair.

Day and night he wept and prayed, and would not be consoled. At last in vision S. Thomas of Canterbury, whom he had so long protected during his life, appeared to him, and bade him make pilgrimage to his tomb. It was an unheard-of thing that a French king should visit England on such an errand, and Louis did not dare to go without consulting his barons. His counsellors warned him of the dangers of the crossing and of trusting himself to the hands of his most powerful enemy. He replied that he did not fear. Three nights the vision was repeated, and Louis determined that nothing should hold him back.

The king started at once on his journey, and sailed from Witsand with Philip of Flanders, Baldwin, count of Guisnes, Henry the Warrior, count of Louvain, and William de Mandeville, earl of Essex, who often negotiated between the French and English kings. He was met at Dover on August 22 by Henry II., and welcomed with "great rejoicing and honour." Thence he went to Canterbury, where he remained two days, passing the night before the martyr's tomb. He made rich offerings at the shrine, and to the monks of Christ Church he gave, by special charter, six hogsheads 'of wine each year, and granted that all they should buy in France should pay no duty. He was himself admitted as a brother of the house, and it was promised that a mass should be said every day for himself and his family. On August 26 he took ship on his return voyage. He found his son recovered.

The journey, to which the chroniclers of the age attach so high a religious importance, was unquestionably a political event of considerable interest. It was accepted by English writers as a pledge that the French king would no longer encourage the insurrections which he had hitherto so often fostered against his great rival. It prepared the way for the cordial relations between Henry and the young Philip which marked the beginning of the new reign.

Louis returned to Paris. Thence he was on his way to S. Denys to return thanks for his son's recovery when he was seized by a new attack of paralysis, and deprived of the use of his right side and of speech. The coronation had already been fixed for All Saints' Day. It was more than ever necessary that it should take place without delay. On October 31 Philip arrived at Rheims. The city was thronged with strangers from all countries. Prominent among them was the young Henry of England, himself crowned during his father's lifetime, nine years before. He brought rich gifts from his father, and did homage to the new king for his fiefs.

On All Saints' Day, in the great cathedral, William, archbishop of Rheims, his uncle, placed the crown upon the young Philip's head. The count of Flanders carried the sword of state, the young Henry of England the crown, which returned to S. Denys when the ceremony was over. Philip was fourteen years two months and ten days old. His father still lay sick, and could not come to the coronation, and his mother remained by her husband's bed.

The new king's first acts were to confirm his father's grants to the monks of Canterbury and his gift of freedom to the serfs of Orleans, which had been declared on the coronation day. For nearly a year King Louis

lingered on. He died on September 18, 1180, and Philip
became sole king. From the hour of his coronation
three parties contended for the direction of the young
sovereign's policy.

First there was the family of his mother. The house
of Champagne, next to the house of Anjou, was at once
the nearest and the greatest of the vassal houses of
France. Thibault V., count of Blois, was also seneschal
of France, and the position still held some of its ancient
privileges and powers. His brother Stephen was
count of Sancerre, his brother William since 1176
archbishop of Rheims, and the eldest of the brothers,
Henry, was count of Champagne. The counts of Blois
and Champagne had each married half-sisters of the
king, the issue of Louis's first marriage. The family
seemed to enclose the king as in a net.

Secondly, there was the busy brain of Henry II. ever
scheming to control, though not to conquer, the power of
his suzerain at Paris. It was the aim of this great king
to surround the French monarch with a ring of his own
states and those of his allies, to confine his action within
narrow limits, and to neutralise, if he could not direct, his
external relations. But in the house of Champagne there
was no man of commanding genius, and Henry had no
desire to control the young king in the exercise of his
internal goverment.

A third party centred round a man abler than any of
the king's uncles, and of more dangerous personal ambition than the English king. Philip of Alsace, count of
Flanders and Vermandois, had already endeavoured to join
forces with the house of Champagne by a double marriage
treaty. His nephew, Baldwin of Hainault, son of his

sister Margaret, should marry the daughter of Henry of
Champagne, while his niece Isabel, sister of the young
Baldwin, should wed Henry, the count of Champagne's
heir.   He had during the earlier years of Henry II. been
constantly his ally, but the alliance was as constantly
broken as it was periodically renewed, and though it
served the purposes of both princes well when it was
necessary to combine against the French king, it was not
based upon any permanent union of interest or policy.
During the later years of Louis VII., Philip of Flanders
had become the most prominent personage at the king's
court.   He had himself taken part in the pilgrimage to
Canterbury.   He had probably already planned with
the king the marriage of the young Philip, which was
to take place after his coronation.   He was himself one
of the greatest of European princes.   He claimed
descent from Charles the Great, and he was a kinsman
of the Emperor Frederic I.   From his county of
Flanders, with his wife's land of Vermandois and the
districts of Amiens and Valois which owned his sway,
he aimed at forming, through the lords of Brabant,
Namur, and Hainault and the great ecclesiastical states,
a network of alliances on the borders of France and the
Empire which should give him something of the position
of a middle kingdom, and enable him to exercise a
decisive influence on the policy of each great power in
turn.   He was an active and ambitious man, and in
ability one of the greatest of the foreigners who
reigned in the Middle Ages over the rich and powerful
towns which made the strength of the little Flemish
state.

The first decisive event which proved the influence

that the count of Flanders had acquired in the direction
of French policy was the marriage of the young king at
Bapaume on April 28, 1180, to Isabel, eldest daughter of
the count of Hainault, and niece of Philip himself.   The
suggested alliance with Champagne gave way before the
far more brilliant prospect of a marriage with the king
of the Franks.   From the French side the match was
warmly supported.   Apart from the influence of the
Flemish count, there were not wanting shrewd politicians to advise the boy-king of the support which it
would give him against the too closely encircling power
of his mother's family.   The chronicle of S. Denys
speaks of the "counsel of certain prudent and wise men
who were about the king," and Gilbert of Mons, writing
from the court of the count of Hainault, repeats the
statement.   Rigord speaks of one adviser in particular,
who has with great probability been identified as
Bernard de Bré, a monk of Grandmont, who during all
the earlier part of the reign exercised considerable
influence over Philip Augustus.

Isabel was beautiful and young.   The marriage, from
the French point of view, was probably the best that the
king could have made, for the count of Flanders was
childless, and he promised that after his death Artois—the
"city of Arras, and S. Omer, and Aire, and Hesdin, that
is, the land beyond the great dyke "—should pass to the
crown of France.   It was more than the chronicler of
Hainault states—Bapaume was included, Ruot, Lens, and
the overlordship of Bologne, S. Pol, Guisnes, and Lille.
But the count of Hainault was a man of honour.   He
had long ago promised his daughter to the young Henry
of Champagne.   It was only by the powerful will of the

count of Flanders that the young bride was taken away.
Baldwin of Hainault, says his chancellor, grieved for the
oath that he had sworn.

The marriage took place on April 28. A month
later, on May 29, the young queen was crowned at S.
Denys, in the presence of her father and her uncle. For
many years the marriage remained childless. Not till
September 5, 1187, did she present the king with a son,
Louis, who lived to succeed his father on the throne,
and whose birth was celebrated, says Rigord, with torch-
light processions for a whole week and ceaseless song
and dance in the streets, and was communicated to the
distant provinces by special messengers announcing
the glad news.

The marriage of Philip Augustus preceded the death
of his father only by five months. During that time
the influence of the count of Flanders was predominant.
He has been somewhat hastily described as the tutor,
guardian, or protector of the king, but though his position of chief adviser may have given him many of the
privileges of guardian, he never formally received such
a title. Louis VII. till his death was counted the true
king. He made no abdication, and his son Philip had
been crowned at an age when custom considered him
capable of ruling in his own person. Before the coronation Louis had charged the count of Flanders to watch
over and advise his son, and the great vassal took
oath faithfully to protect and to instruct his young
lord.

Philip as joint king had by custom the same powers
as his father, but they were powers enjoyed only by the
favour of the actual sovereign. The heads of father and

son, with the same legend, appeared on either side of the coinage struck at Laon in the year 1180. The illness of his father suffered much of the real power to pass into Philip's hands, but he spoke of the old king in at least one formal document as his "lord, the king of the Franks." From the very first he was thrust into political entanglements of complexity that might have baffled a wiser head. We have every reason to suppose that though he took advice, he was almost from the first the guiding spirit in affairs. His powerful mind and strong character were formed by the pressure of affairs. He became a man of business, and a royal man of business was in the Middle Ages made to be a great king.

With his young wife and her uncle, with Robert Clement, Ralph of Clermont, the constable, and the other advisers of the old king by his side, Philip, with care and discretion, surveyed the political engagements in which his kingdom was involved, and prepared to strike out a decisive line of action for himself. At his right hand stood the great warrior and statesman whose niece he had married. But the influence of the count of Flanders was not uncontested. The claims of a queen-mother had always been recognised in French history as considerable. By virtue of unction and coronation, she was a real participator in the sovereignty. Alice of Champagne was by no means ready to surrender her prerogatives. Still less were her brothers willing to see the influence of their house extinguished by the uncle of the new king's wife. Philip of Flanders had been somewhat too hasty in allowing his assumption of power over the young king to be marked by a direct attack on the queen his mother. The king had taken from her her dower lands, unwilling, says a chronicler, that she should have in her hands the castles that belonged to the estates. It was an attempt, no doubt, to secure the king against a movement of the house of Champagne. It is asserted that the queen left her sick husband and fled. A few weeks in any case brought forward her wrongs through a powerful champion. Henry II. determined to throw his weight into the scale against Philip of Flanders.

Events indeed had marched rapidly under the young king. The English chroniclers already spoke of him as a tyrant who, under the advice of the count of Flanders, had rejected the counsel of his father's friends, and treated them with contempt and hatred. They had appealed, says one of the officials of Henry's court, directly to the English king against the evil machinations of the Fleming. Henry, the younger, crossed over to England in March to warn his father of the danger that was growing in France. They returned to Normandy together, and the French queen, with her brother, Count Thibault, sought in person the advice and assistance of the great Angevin. It was a curious reversal of what had often happened in the last twenty years. The French court had often supported Henry's rebellious sons, and had in 1173 offered shelter to his intriguing wife, herself once the wife of the French king. Now Henry II. gave support and counsel to Louis's third queen against her son. Philip, with all the hot eagerness of youth, brought an army to the Norman frontier. Henry was there before him. The young king's marriage intervened, and a few months later both sovereigns were in more peaceable mood.

Philip had already shown all a boy's eagerness for

martial exploits, and he had signalised the beginning of
his reign, like his grandfather, by repressing the outrages of those who maltreated the Church.　He was
no less prepared to meet attack from his mother and
her kin.　He obtained three thousand footmen from
Baldwin of Hainault.　He was prepared for war, but he
was too sagacious not to see that peace was more to his
interest.　The English king was seeking in the spring
of 1180 to form an alliance in support of his son-in-law,
Henry the Lion of Saxony, who had been disseised of
his vast possessions by the Emperor Frederic.　On May
14 the Saxon duke defeated Bernard of Anhalt, on
whom Saxony had been conferred.　It seemed probable
that he would win back his possessions.　His father-in-
law prepared to enter into an alliance with the young
French king at the expense of the Flemish count, whose
support he would otherwise have been anxious to
secure.　Philip of France, he thought, would give the
most important aid to the coalition against the emperor.
With his own aims, and the interests of the house of
Champagne in view, Henry met the young French king
at the famous meeting-place, between Gisors and Trie-
Château, on the banks of the Epte.

A great dyke marked the frontier between Normandy
and France.　It was overlooked by the strong castle of
Gisors, part of the dowry which had been given by
Louis VII. when his daughter Margaret married the
young Henry of England.　On June 28 the two kings met.
It was probably the first occasion on which they had
stood face to face.　It can hardly be that the great
English monarch, renowned throughout Europe as a
warrior and statesman, could have foreseen that the deli-

cate boy, who less than a year before had seemed likely to
die while still a child, would one day beat him at his
own weapons of war and craft, and would win back
from his sons the mighty heritage of the Norman dukes
and the demon race of Anjou.   They met now as a hot
youth listening with respect to the wise counsel of the
greatest of his vassals and one of the most famous of
European kings.   The old king—for so men already
began to call him, though he was but forty-seven—used
both fair and bitter words.   The boy was perhaps
already eager to be rid of the controlling hand of his
wife's uncle.   Before the end of the day he had turned
from the advice of the count of Flanders and Robert
Clement and promised to be reconciled to his mother
and her house.   A treaty was drawn up and confirmed
by the oath of both kings, which laid the foundation
for a new and peaceable relation between the two
kingdoms.

The treaty began by renewing that of Ivry, concluded
between Henry of England and " my lord Louis, the king
of the Franks " in 1177.   It declared that the two kings
were, and would remain, friends, and would protect each
other in life and limb and earthly honour against all
men.   Neither would demand aught of the other's land
from henceforth, save only in the case of Auvergne or
the fief of Châteauroux, or in the little fiefs in Berry,
matters still in dispute ; and the disputed claims, if the
king could not agree on them, should be submitted to
the arbitration of three bishops and three barons nominated by each king.   Philip at once nominated the
bishops of Clermont, Nevers, and Troyes, and his uncles
Thibault of Blois, Robert of Dreux, and Pierre of

Courtenay ; and any further dispute that should arise
was to be submitted to the judgment of the same men.
The treaty concluded with the most solemn vows of
mutual loyalty.   Henry II., warrior though he was, was
never eager for war.   It is possible that he may have
sincerely intended to arrange all future disputes in this
strangely modern manner, but he had to reckon with the
hot blood of a young king in whose heart burnt relentless hatred to the Angevins.

For the time all looked well.   Henry wrote a letter to
his justiciar, Ranulf Glanville, announcing the happy
reconciliation that he had made, with some very pious
expressions of gratitude for the Christian feeling that
had been shown by all.   Philip took again into favour
the whole house of Champagne, including Duke Henry of
Burgundy and Henry, count of Bar-le-Duc, nephews of
Queen Alice.   He assigned to his mother seven livres
parisis a day so long as Louis VII. should live, and after
his death he promised her her whole dower, keeping only
the strong castles in his own hand.   Philip of Flanders
entered into the arrangement.   He renewed his former
treaties with Henry, and promised to supply him at need
with five hundred knights in return for an annual pension
of a hundred pounds.   The French constable, Ralph of
Clermont, did homage to Henry II.   It was a kind of
final ratification of the peace.   Then the kings went
their ways.

The treaty marked the downfall of the predominance
of Flanders in the counsels of the French sovereign.   It
marked a temporary *rapprochement* with England.   But
its importance may easily be exaggerated.   Philip ceased
his unseemly quarrel with his mother and her kin, but

he did not give them any real power of control over
himself. He took the advice of Henry II., but he
showed no sign of assisting his designs in Germany.

The young king now turned to the serious question
which had for so long beset every French king at his
accession—the ravaging forays of the baronage against
unprotected churches and abbeys. In December 1179
the churches of Berry had cried out against Hebes VI.
of Charenton. He was compelled to submit entirely to
the king's will, to give satisfaction to the churches, and
promise better conduct in the future. Another expedition followed. Humbert III. of Beaujeu, William III.,
count of Châlon-sur-Saône, Giraud, count of Vienne,
and other "sons of iniquity" were robbing and attacking the abbey of Cluny, the church of Mâcon, and the
neighbouring churches and monasteries. Philip marched
into the district, and repressed the wrongdoers with a
firm hand. In September 1180 he was at the castle of
Pierre-Perthuis, near Vézelay. He presided at a royal
court, in which the grievance of the church of Mâcon
against Count Gerard of Vienne was heard. The judgment was wholly against the count. He was allowed no
fortified place within the area of the church's privilege, and the clergy were allowed to fortify the church
and their houses. A little later the count of Châlon
came to the young king at Lens and submitted to his
decision. The royal army had compelled obedience.
The new reign was begun well. "Thus," cries the enthusiastic Breton clerk whose poem describes the king's
progress from the cradle to the grave, "the new king con-
secrated devoutly to Christ and His Church the first-fruits
of his works and his first fightings : thus, a new knight,

he loved rather to defend with his arms the patrimony of Christ than to turn himself to the vain sports of chivalry." New knight he was — made, it has been suggested, by Philip of Flanders at the great tournament held at Arras on Whit Sunday 1180. He was now fifteen years old, and had been married four months. On September 19 his father died, and he became sole king in name as well as in reality.

The last months of Louis VII. had been spent at the monastery of Barbeaux, at Fontaine-le-Port; but as he felt his death draw nigh he was moved to Paris. There, with the help of the bishop and the heads of the great abbeys of the diocese, he divided all his money and precious articles among the poor. He called his son to his bed—so says Giraldus, generally very well informed as to French history—and warned him in the very article of death that he should reclaim with all his power the rights of the crown, and, above all, that he should recover Auvergne, concerning which great wrong had been done. This he charged him as he valued his blessing. Thus, with a command which opened again the war with the Angevins that he himself had never had skill or courage to carry to a successful issue, he passed away. He left directly to his son a heritage of war.

He was buried at Barbeaux on September 21. The immediate consequences of his death were but slight. It was not till eight years later that his son was able to carry out his last wishes by the conquest of Auvergne. Now he merely confirmed in a meeting with Henry II. the treaty that he had made three months before.

At the beginning of the next year, January 1181, he showed that he was still ready to learn from the English

king, for when Henry issued his assize of arms at Le
Mans requiring all who had £25 Angevin in chattels
to provide themselves with hauberk, lance, and sword,
and all others with lesser arms—an edict intended to
arm the whole population—Philip as well as the count
of Flanders issued similar ordinances for their own
domains. On April 27 the two kings met at Gué S.
Rémy, near Nonancourt, in friendly conference, and
Henry departed to England with an assurance that his
dominions were safe in his absence.

How far the house of Champagne was yet fully
reconciled to the king is doubtful, for the march of
Philip across the Loire and his capture of the castle of
Châtillon, and subsequent pardon of his uncle, Count
Stephen of Sancerre, which the chroniclers attribute to
this year, may have taken place before the reconciliation
in 1180. In any case the appearance of a French king
with a victorious army south of the Loire was a sign
that a new era had set in for the monarchy. But his
power was not long uncontested. Philip of Flanders,
disgusted at finding that his influence over the young
king had entirely ceased, formed an alliance with Hugh
of Burgundy, with the house of Champagne itself, and
with the counts of Namur and Hainault, and invaded
France. Philip applied in urgent haste to Henry II.,
and to his intrepidity and tact he owed the preservation
of his power. At Gisors the English king met young
Philip and the count of Flanders, and arranged at
length a peace between them.

Again, at the end of the year, war broke out.
The count of Flanders attacked his old ally, Ralph,
count of Clermont, and devastated his land.   The French

king received aid from the young Henry of England,
and the invasion was checked for a while.   "The
chief and principal cause of this war," says the English
chronicler, with sagacity, "was that Philip, king of
France, spurning the counsel of his kinsfolk, adhered to
Henry, king of England; whence it came about that
William, archbishop of Rheims, and Count Thibault and
Count Stephen, finding that they were despised, strove
to rise against their nephew, the king." Stephen of
Sancerre had actually done homage to the count of
Flanders.   The king seized his lands, and, on the advice
of the constable, Ralph of Clermont, refused to restore
them.   Thus the influence of the house of Anjou and
the advice of Ralph of Clermont were now predominant
in the counsels of King Philip.

A further cause of contest with Flanders soon arose.
On March 26, 1183, Isabella, wife of Philip of Flanders,
and countess of Vermandois in her own right, died.
Philip at once claimed that, as she had no direct male
heirs, Vermandois lapsed to the French crown.   He
claimed also Artois and the district of Amiens, promised
to him on his marriage.   Again Henry II. mediated
when war was actually in progress.   Amiens was
promised immediately, and the promise of Artois was
renewed.   But neither promise was kept.   In 1184
Philip of Flanders married again, and the prospect of a
new line to cut him off from the succession to the
Flemish fiefs stirred Philip to immediate action.

He mustered a large army at Compiègne, marched
on Amiens, besieged Boves, and carried all before him.
Gilbert of Mons, from the side of the vanquished,
estimated his force, with pardonable exaggeration, at 2000

knights and 140,000 men-at-arms, while the count of
Flanders, he said, could bring but 400 knights and
40,000 foot-men into the field. The course of the war is
less questionable. The young French king had been preparing during the whole of his reign for a trial of
strength, and his troops proved all that he had expected.
To this campaign belongs a curious story which
Giraldus tells to illustrate his passionate determination
and its effect on his barons.

"In the early part of his reign," he says, "when his
blessed father had been some time taken from this
world of ours and the youth himself was still of tender
years, he assembled the army of France at Amiens to
oppose Count Philip of Flanders, who, on the death,
without children or heir, of the countess, his wife, and
heiress to the count of Vermandois, ventured to hold
possession of that countship. The forces were gathered
together and prepared to meet in hostile conflict, when
the barons of France, thinking with the poet that the
wise man ought first to try every weapon, with one
consent expressed the opinion that a peaceful solution
of the difficulty should be sought, for the count, a
man of vast resources and great influence, had many
enthusiastic supporters who had been drawn to his side
by his entreaties or bribes, by the claims of affection or
kinship. The leading men accordingly met to consider
the question, while the king withdrew apart for a time,
and sat holding a green hazel wand in his hand or
gnawing it with his teeth, at the same time glancing
keenly about him. On the barons observing this, and
marking with wonder the youth's attitude and gestures,
one of them declared that he would bestow a gallant

steed on the man who could disclose the prince's medita-
tions. Hearing this, a certain prattling fellow immediately
sped to the king with the earnest prayer that by reveal-
ing the thoughts of his mind he would confer on him, as
if a present from himself, the steed which had been
promised on such conditions. The king, to whom the
man was not unknown, thereupon unfolded the secrets
of his mind. 'I was wondering,' he said, 'whether at
some future date God will ever think fit to bestow
on me or some other king of the Franks this favour—
the restoration of the realm of France to its former
position, to the extent and the renown which it once
enjoyed in the days of Charles.' When this had been
reported to the barons and the steed given according to
the promise, with one voice they all instantly burst
forth into these words: 'Perish the man who throws
any obstacle in the path of such a prince, with a mind
so nobly bent on the recovery of his kingdom's rights.
By God's aid, neither in these rights nor in any others
shall he ever meet with failure.' Thus it came about
that the splendid countship of Vermandois, after the
humiliation of its powerful holder, was, with all its
wealthy towns, placed in the hands of King Philip, while
still a youth, without difficulty, delay, or any warlike
contest."

Such determination carried all before it. During a
great part of the summer the two armies watched each
other along the frontier line. The French king lay
for three weeks before Boves, and Rigord records a
fantastic miracle, by which the fields trodden down by
his horsemen bore a double harvest, whereas those
where the Flemings had camped remained bare and

barren.   Philip of Flanders was obliged humbly to
submit.   Again the intervention of Henry II. was
sought.   Peace was concluded at Aumâle on November
7, 1185, in the presence of the English king and the
archbishops of Cologne and Rennes.   Vermandois was
at once yielded, with the district of Amiens, while
Péronne, S. Quentin, and the whole of Artois were to
pass to the king after the count's death.

Philip had won his first signal triumph, his first
great accession of territory.   His victory had been due
to diplomacy as well as force.   The count of Flanders
had applied for help to the emperor, ready to play one
suzerain against the other, and the question had become
complicated with the long struggle of Henry the Lion
to regain his lands.   In the autumn of 1184 the emperor
had pardoned Henry, and the peace of Aumâle was in
one aspect a result of that reconciliation.   England, the
Empire, Flanders, and France came together again in
something like an universal peace.

Peace with Flanders did not free the young king
from active military effort.   He turned to redress the
wrongs of the Burgundians.   Hugh of Vergy called
for his aid against the attack of Duke Hugh.   Philip,
bringing the count of Flanders with him, delivered the
castle, which, says one chronicler, had undergone a three
years' siege.   The deliverance was paid for by a recognition on the part of the count that he held his fief
directly from the crown.   But Hugh of Burgundy was
not yet conquered.   The churches cried out against his
tyranny, and called in the pious French king against
their godless duke.   Philip thrice solemnly warned him,
then marched against his castle of Châtillon-sur-Seine,

took it, and compelled the duke to restore all that he
had taken, to redress the wrongs, and be reconciled to
the Church. He returned to Paris in triumph. Thus
briefly may be sketched the progress of the young conqueror in the north. But these events had not obscured
the important changes which had taken place in the
relations of the French king with the house of Anjou.

On the death of Louis, Philip renewed the treaty
which he had signed three months before, but it was
not long before he allowed his real feelings to appear.
In January 1181 the two kings had met and promised
succour to the Holy Land. In the summer, Henry had
again intervened to make peace between Philip and
the count of Flanders, and again after Easter in the
next year. The young French king accepted his aid
during these years with an easy cynicism, but he never
ceased to watch for the opportunity of repudiating all
his obligations. The last years of the treacherous young
Henry, his repeated struggles with his father and his
brother, all told in favour of the French. Philip did
not actively intervene, but when the wretched father
was still mourning over his unhappy son, he came
forward to demand the dower and portion of his sister
Margaret, who had returned to him some weeks before
her husband's death. Gisors, the chief town of the
Norman Vexin, the rich plain which was ever a debate-
able land between the French king and the Norman
duke, was the main object of Philip's demand, and often
did he meet Henry at the great oak of conference
between Gisors and Troye, "but in nothing could they
agree." At the end of the year 1183 Henry did homage
in his own person to Philip—an act which he had

avoided year after year on many skilful pretexts—for
all his lands over sea, and Philip accepted a yearly
payment in lieu of Margaret's dower, on the understanding that Gisors should now be the dowry of his
sister Alais, who had been promised years before as bride
to Richard, Henry's second son, who still lived under
ward at Winchester, and who was again pledged to one
of Henry's sons " whom he will." In 1184 he accepted
Henry's mediation with Flanders about Vermandois,
and again, a year later, English envoys intervened
between them. The year passed by without contest,
and early in 1186 the two kings met at Gisors and
renewed their promises of peace. All the while he
was plotting with one of Henry's treacherous sons.
Geoffrey, whose wife Constance was countess of Brittany,
was easily led to ally himself with the French king,
a remoter suzerain than his father. He went to Paris,
and his winning manners won the hearts of king and
barons alike. Unanimously, says Giraldus, he was
chosen seneschal of France; and the plot against
the old king was nearly ripe when a fever, following
on an accident in a tournament, it would seem, carried
him off on August 19, 1186. Philip ordered him to
be buried before the altar of Notre Dame, and in the
agony of his grief would have flung himself into the
grave of his dead friend had not the bystanders held
him back. Such was the fascination of the young
prince whom Gerald calls the Ulysses of the Angevins :
but Philip's grief did not obscure his ulterior aims. He
at once demanded the wardship of his friend's little
daughter, who was, till the birth of a posthumous son,
March 29, 1187, his only child. Henry put off the

demand and avoided a war, which the discovery of the
building of a castle near Gisors by Philip nearly pro-
voked.   In the summer of 1187 Philip won over
Richard, who made long sojourn with him, and " whom
he so honoured that by day they ate at one table, off
one dish, and at night they slept in one bed.   And the
king of France loved him as his own soul."   Whereat,
adds the English chronicler, King Henry was greatly
alarmed, wondering what it should portend.   He was
not kept long in doubt.   In September Richard seized
the treasure at Chinon, and fled into Poitou to raise
an insurrection against his father.   Yet again Henry
brought him to submit, and to repent that he had
followed evil counsellors who would sow discord between them.

At the beginning of the next year Philip demanded
that Alais should marry Richard, or Gisors be restored
to him.   The crusade, and the piteous appeals of pope
and patriarch, prevented war.   The kings solemnly laid
aside their feuds and took the cross.   The archbishop
of Tyre came to them as they met by the tree of conference, and turned their hearts, to the great joy of all
the host.   Crowds ran to take the holy sign : the crusade,
it might seem, was begun.

The next few months were spent in making preparation and ordinances for the expedition.   Even then,
however, the fiery impetuosity of Richard could not be
restrained.   He was using the time of waiting by paying
off old scores against the count of Toulouse, and Philip
complained to Henry, who could neither justify nor
control his son.   Philip took occasion thereupon to invade Berry, which was part of the heritage of Eleanor of

Aquitaine.   Châteauroux opened its gates to him, and he took all the castles except Loches and those in the royal demesne.   Buchard of Vendôme, who had already acted with the young Henry against his father, now went over to Philip.   Richard too now sent word to his father that all he had done was by Philip's consent.   The net was closing round the old king.

On June 16, 1188, Archbishop Baldwin of Canterbury was sent to King Philip to pacify him, but without result. Then Henry sent his youngest and well-beloved son John, and in July he crossed himself to Barfleur.   Richard was now turning his arms against Philip, driving his men from Berry and ravaging the lands of the barons who had adhered to him; and Philip himself was forced to guard his own lands against "the old lion," whom he still feared.   His warlike and unclerkly cousin, the bishop of Beauvais (Philip, son of Robert, count of Dreux, who held the see from 1180 to 1217), was wasting the Norman frontier.   Philip responded to the demands of Henry for reparation by answering that he would not desist till all Berry and all the Norman Vexin were his. Thereupon Henry himself invaded France, and advanced to Mantes, and his Welch troops burnt many castles and villages, and, "sparing no man, slew all whom they found."   Philip's offers of peace were now rejected, and in rage he cut down the famous tree of conference, "a certain very beautiful elm between Gisors and Trye."

Further conferences between the kings were in-effectual.   Richard was already turning towards the French king—perhaps had always been in his secrets. At length, on November 18, after another meeting between Soligny and Bonsmoulins, when Philip offered to restore all he had taken if Alais should be married at once to Richard and the king would recognise Richard as the heir to all his lands, the quarrel between father and son became irreconcilable, and Richard did homage to Philip for all the continental lands of his house. Papal legates in vain tried to mediate a peace. Short truces were made, but the inevitable conflict could not be long postponed.

Philip had indeed every reason for his determination that the disputes should be decisively settled. The piteous cries of the Christian kingdom in the East were again and again renewed. But it would have been impossible for him to leave his lands when Henry remained—as he certainly would have done—in Europe. Family honour too imperatively demanded that he should see his sister Alais wedded : dark stories were whispered that Henry could not give her to his son because he had himself done her foul wrong.

At the end of May 1189 Philip, Henry, and Richard met, near la Ferté, Bernard, in the presence of John of Anagni, the pope's legate. Philip's demands were the marriage of Alais, the recognition of Richard as heir, and that John, whom Richard saw now to be his rival in his father's affection, should go on the crusade. Richard declared that he would not himself go to Jerusalem unless his brother went with him.

Still Henry thought himself the greatest king in Christendom, and he would not yield. The legate declared that unless Philip would agree to peace he would lay his land under interdict. But Philip answered, in words which English chroniclers recorded with something of a genuine sympathy, that it did not belong to

the Roman Church to lay censures on the realm of
France if the king of France avenged his wrongs and the
honour of his crown on his rebellious vassals. " And
he added that the legate had scented Henry's money."

The end was now come. Henry summoned aid from
England. Philip poured his troops into Maine. On
June 12 he surprised Henry in Le Mans. Burning
the suburbs, he surrounded the city with a wall of flame.
Henry's men tried to break down the bridge, but the
French knights rushed upon them as they were at
work, and, driving them back, entered the town in con-
fused *mêlée* with them. Then Henry fled. The French
carried all before them. The citadel of Le Mans surrendered, and castle after castle followed. On July 3 Tours
yielded. Already it was clear that the French king had
won a decisive triumph. Henry had scarce resisted : he
was lying down to die. The great vassals of the French
crown had some pity for the old man in his fall. On
July 2 Philip of Flanders, William, archbishop of
Rheims, and Hugh III., duke of Burgundy, went to him,
as he lay at Saumur, to beg him to submit. They went,
says the chronicler significantly, by their own will, not
Philip's.

On July 4 (but the date is not certain), at Colombières
near Villandri on the Cher, the two kings met, and there
Henry yielded to all Philip's demands. He did homage,
he promised to surrender Alais and to allow her marriage,
to make his barons do fealty to Richard, to pay 20,000
marks, and to start for the crusade in the middle of the
next Lent. It was a complete submission. Two days
later the greatest of the Angevins was dead.

Philip had triumphed as none of his race had done

before him. The greatest statesman and warrior of Europe had knelt at his feet. He was for the moment the unquestioned lord of his great kingdom. But the victory was greater in appearance than in reality. Philip had no time to use the fruits of his success. It was impossible in common decency any longer to delay the crusade. He had proved his ability. He had not established his power.

In the great struggle against the English king a pressing claim, which both Henry and Philip had long formally recognised, had been put aside. As early as 1181 Philip had promised succour to the Holy Land. In 1185 Henry had received the keys of Jerusalem from the hands of the patriarch, and had consulted with the French king about an immediate crusade. Mutual jealousies had soon disturbed the agreement, and for two years more nothing was done.

The sharp contentions of the year 1187 were interrupted by the news of the Christian disasters in Palestine. Internal dissensions, the feebleness of the monarchs, and the growth of the strong power of Saladin had year by year brought nearer the inevitable destruction of the kingdom of Jerusalem. On May 1, 1187, the Templars and Hospitallers were defeated at Nazareth. On July 3 Saladin took Tiberias, and next day, at the battle of Hattin, the Christian army was surrounded, King Guy made prisoner, and the true cross taken. Letters from the Templars and from the Genoese, who had early intelligence, reached Europe before long. Jerusalem, Ascalon, Tyre, and Beyrout alone held out, and Beyrout fell on August 6. Urban III. died of grief, men said. His successor, Gregory

VIII., urged all Christian princes to lay aside their dissensions and unite to save what still remained of the Holy Land. But before his letters were written the worst misfortunes had come to pass. Jerusalem itself was besieged on September 20, and on October 3 Saladin entered the Holy City in triumph.

The terrible news reached Europe before the end of the month, and at last roused the Christian kings. Gregory VIII. held the papal throne but two months. At his death Clement III. succeeded, and pressed on the crusade with all his energy. The archbishop of Tyre (perhaps the famous historian of the kingdom of Jerusalem) preached with a fervour which turned the thoughts of multitudes to the East. The impulsive Richard of Poitou was the first to take the cross. Philip was not so soon stayed from his own projects. He renewed his claim to Gisors, and insisted on the long-delayed marriage of his sister. But a conference in January 1188 proved an opportunity which the archbishop of Tyre did not neglect, and the French and English kings, "at his preaching and by God's help, on that day were made friends, and took the cross from his hands." The French chose red crosses for their badge, as the English chose white and the Flemings green. Both kings published ordinances for the collection of a tithe of all property, in which movables as well as revenues were taxed. The French ordinance differed somewhat from the English—mainly in the omission of a provision for the assessment of the value of the goods of those who were believed to have offered too small a sum, by the oath of a jury. The French crusaders were to have two years' respite for payment of their debts. Wherever

a lord had the right of capital jurisdiction he was to
have the right to receive all that his men had contributed.
The tithe for the Holy War was to take precedence of
all debts.   Laymen were bound by oath to pay it, clergy
by threat of excommunication. Landless knights were
to pay from their movables to their lord, or if they had
no lord, to the lord of the district in which they lived.
If a young lord took the cross while his parents did
not, he was given the right to exact a tithe from their
property.   The continental system of which Philip's
ordinance is typical makes the lord enforce the payment.
In England the coercive power lies with the public
authorities.   Such were Philip's preparations.

But it took more than the preparations for a crusade
to divert Philip from his plan, and it needed but the
slight excuse of a chance fray in Toulouse and a quarrel
between Count Raymond and Richard to embroil him
again with the Angevin house.   From June 1188,
when the war broke out again—in spite of the pope's
intervention, and the Emperor Frederic's departure for
the East,—till the great King Henry's death, July 6,
1189, all thought of crusade was laid aside.   Not till
Philip found himself at length the conqueror of the
house he had so long determined to destroy did he
remember his vow to succour the Christians of the East.
His interests could not suffer by his absence if he took
Richard with him.   The Frankish lands were in
unwonted peace.   Philip had all to gain by a season of
quiet in the land.   He called then upon the English
king and his barons to join him in his journey to the
holy fields.

The crusade was but an episode in the career of

Philip Augustus, but it was an episode with which he could not dispense. Like the great Elector in Carlyle's description, he had "his reasonable private aim sun-clear to him all the while"; but he could not afford to despise any of the necessary trappings of a great medieval monarch. Moral greatness was respected at least as highly in the twelfth as it is in the nineteenth century, and Philip eagerly sought the fame of a devoted son of the Church. Nor could he easily have held back when all the great monarchs of Europe caught the enthusiasm of the Holy War. No king was ever more truly a man of his age than he, and the strongest appeal to the imagination and self-devotion of the men of his day was the cry that the sepulchre of the Lord was once more in the hands of the infidels.

Philip undertook his crusade with the same shrewd providence with which he entered upon all his under-takings. He did not neglect the religious or the ceremonial aspects of the call. He went in state to S. Denys, and received "most devoutly" the pilgrim's scrip and staff from the hand of the archbishop, William of Rheims, his uncle. He met Richard at S. Rémy, near Nonancourt, on July 4, 1190, and signed a treaty of peace, an alliance with him in which both promised to defend each other's lands as they would their own. Most important of all, he drew up, in the presence of "his household and his friends," his personal testament and his order for the government of the realm. It was a constitutional document of the first importance, and the opportunity of the crusade was happily taken to avoid the disturbances which its articles would under ordinary circumstances inevitably have caused. On

July 1, 1190, the two kings met at Vezelai with
"innumerable hosts," and the carnal side of their
expedition showed itself clearly enough, for they agreed
to divide equally all that they should gain in the war
—a bargain which led to much of the strife that marred
their campaign. Then the great armies marched to Lyons
together, where they separated, Richard sailing from
Marseilles, and Philip from Genoa. The French king,
delicate from his youth, had already begun to suffer from
the toils of the expedition, and he lay for some days
sick at Genoa, where Richard visited him. From the
Genoese he was to obtain his transports, and he agreed
with them to supply succour in men and arms while
he was in Palestine, paying them five thousand eight
hundred and sixty marks of silver for the aid. He
sailed a few days later, and reached Messina on September 16, with one ship, entering the city with no pomp,
and being received with open arms by Tancred, the
claimant of the Sicilian crown, who was eager for
recognition by the Western powers. In the political
troubles of the Sicilian kingdom it would perhaps have
been wise not to interfere, and indeed Philip took no
greater part than he could help. He declined the offer
of Tancred's daughter in marriage, but he did enough to
arouse the suspicion of the emperor, Henry VI. The
crusaders were robbed right and left in the island, the
chroniclers say, and because Philip suffered it while
Richard punished, the former was called by the Greeks
"the Lamb," and the latter "the Lion." The English
writers accused Philip of disloyalty to Richard. He
could hardly be expected to take much interest in the
claims of the English king to his widowed sister's dowry,

but it seems clear that, though he did not take part in the capture of Messina, his relations with the English remained friendly, and his mediation secured peace between Richard and Tancred. A slight quarrel there was when Richard wished to set up his banners on the walls of Messina, October 4; but four days later the two kings "swore on the relics of the saints to keep good faith to one another, both as regards their own persons and the two armies, during their pilgrimage."

Christmas they spent together in amity, and from day to day tournaments diverted the knights while they waited for favourable winds. It was then that Richard's hot temper burst out against William de Barres, the gallant French knight who had been his prisoner two years before, and was afterwards to save Philip's life at Bouvines. The French knight was more than a match for the English king in tilting, and it needed Philip's personal intercession to win forgiveness for his follower's prowess. Tancred, it seemed, was not unwilling to keep the two kings from any close friendship, and there was still the question of Richard's marriage with Alais. This was at last settled before Philip sailed for Acre, and the claims of the unhappy lady to be queen of England were at last abandoned even by her brother.

It was on Saturday, March 30, 1191, that Philip at length set sail from Messina, and three weeks later he arrived at Acre. The weary knights rejoiced, says William the Breton, to leap upon the sand by the walls of the great city which he calls Acharon. The siege had been in progress for a year and a half, and Guy de Lusignan had been joined by many of the crusaders.

The besieged were hard pressed, Saladin was unable to relieve them, and it seemed as if the coming of Philip would at once restore the city to the Christians. As soon as he arrived he mounted his horse and rode round the whole of the works of the besieging force. "It is strange," he said, "with so many warriors here, that the town has been so long in taking." He pitched his tent so near the walls that "the enemies of Christ often shot their quarrels and arrows right up to it, and even beyond," and he at once set his engines to work against the fortifications.

Richard did not reach Acre till June, and the French chroniclers say that Philip could have taken the town long before, if he had not wished the English to share in the glory of its capture. The forces had increased almost weekly, and "there was no man of great power or fame who did not come sooner or later to the siege of Acre." Still the siege lingered. Philip fell sick of the strange disease with which the crusaders were so often afflicted. He was wasted with fever, lost his hair and his nails, and was long before he could rise again from his bed. It was not until July 12 that the city surrendered. Philip took possession of the house of the Templars, and Richard, with his young wife, entered the palace, which had of recent years been a favourite residence of the kings of Jerusalem. The stern Saracens passed out from the town, calm as if they were themselves the victors, and the Christian knights marvelled at their cheerful looks.

The capture of Acre ended the hollow amity between the kings which the crusade had begun. It had already been greatly disturbed. The count of Flanders had warned King Philip that Richard was plotting against him. Now the land was, it seemed, again to be in Christian hands, rival claimants again contended for the throne, and while Richard supported Guy, the widower of Queen Sibylla, Philip favoured the claim of Isabella, her sister, and her new husband, Conrad of Montferrat. Again the quarrel was patched up. Guy was to be king for his life, and Conrad was to succeed him. Philip was heartily sick of the war. His son Louis had been grievously ill in France. He was himself still weak and ailing. He had never been enthusiastic about the cause, though even the English chronicler admits that "he had worked well at the siege, and spent money, and given good help, so that he was rightly deemed the most powerful of Christian kings." The death of Philip of Flanders at Acre in June 1191 gave him the chance he had long desired. He determined at once to return and enforce his claim on the lands of his dead wife's father. He wrote from Acre in June to the nobles of the district of Peronne claiming his right of succession to Peronne, and charged the archbishop of Rheims and others to receive the oath of fealty from his new vassals. He had been but four months in the Holy Land. He had taken part in no military operations except those of the siege. Never did a crusading king so lightly perform his vow. But protests were of no avail, and he sailed on July 31.

A beautiful story is told of his homeward voyage. They were off the coast of Pamphylia, and a great storm held them for a day and night. When the knights clustered round the king telling him all was lost, he asked what hour it was. "Midnight," they answered.

" Fear not then," said Philip, " for at this hour the monks in our land are awake, and pray God for us." He landed at Brindisi, and visited Celestine III. at Rome. Men said that he had begged absolution from his oath not to attack the lands of Richard. An English chronicler has preserved the record of his route. He went by Sutri, Viterbo, Montefiascone, Santa Christina, Acquapendente, Radicofani, San Quirico, Buonconvento, Sienna, Castel Fiorentino, Lucca, Capriola, San Lionardo, Luna, Sarzana, Villa Franca, Pontremoli. Monte Barduno—" where Tuscany ends and Italy begins,"—thence by Cassio, Fornuovo, San Donnino, Fiorensuola, Piacenza, to Pavia. The emperor lay hard by at Milan. They met, and Philip, having promised to give no support to Tancred, did his best to incense Henry against Richard. Thence he continued his journey by Mortara, Robbio, Vercelli, and the valley of Maurienne, and so re-entered France. Before the end of the year he was at home. He spent Christmas at Fontevrault, where the tomb of his greatest adversary might well serve to inspire him with new plans of aggression against the Angevin house.

So the king's crusade ended. He had discharged his vow, and came back with some at least of the honour of a loyal Christian and son of the Church. He had won, too, fresh laurels as a soldier. Even the jealous Englishmen, who always accused him of treachery and avarice, acknowledged that he could fight and that he could lead. And his power had not suffered by his absence. He came back to find himself even stronger than when he went away, and with new fields opening before his energetic ambition.

CHAPTER III

THE FALL OF THE ANGEVINS

THE death of Henry II. had done something to redress the balance which his defeat had cast in favour of the young Frankish king. The conquest of so mighty a monarch as he who had set popes at defiance, resisted the will of the Roman emperor, sent his daughters in marriage to Saxony, to Sicily, and to Castile, made leagues with Italian cities, with Spanish monarchs, with chiefs of the Goidels and kings of the far north, and been sought out in all Christendom as the one warrior who was worthy to hold the keys of the Tower of David and of the Holy Sepulchre, was a glory which set Philip high among the mighty princes of his age. But when Henry was dead the practical results of the victory were seen to be small. The twenty thousand marks which Henry had promised were not paid, the castles which were to be held by Philip and Richard jointly were for the most part already in Richard's hands, and he succeeded to the hereditary feud. From the moment of Henry's death Richard took up a new position of hostility to the ally with whose aid he had brought his father to his end. All his

father's servants who had been faithful he retained and
rewarded, but those who had aided in his own rebellion
he contemned and punished.   Such conduct could
hardly imply friendliness to the French king.

There still remained the question of Alais.   Philip
insisted that the marriage should take place.   Richard
was not yet strong enough to refuse it.   On S. Mary
Magdalen's Day, within three weeks of the old king's
death, the king of the English met the king of the
Franks at Gisors.   Philip claimed that town and the
fertile plain around it.   But peace was not yet broken.
Richard pledged himself to pay four thousand marks
besides the twenty thousand his father had promised;
the marriage was to take place, and the claim was to
lie by.   All that Philip had won in fight from Henry
was to go back to Richard, save only his gains in Auvergne
and Berry.   It was little more than a truce, but both
princes were sworn to the crusade, and all Christendom
would have cried out upon them if they had now stayed
to fight at home when the holy city was in the hands of
the infidel.

A few weeks passed, the treaties of perpetual friendship were renewed, and the kings started on their
sacred quest.   How they fared and how little the
traditional quarrel of the houses was appeased by the
progress of the Holy War we have already seen.   Philip
parted with Richard indeed with the semblance of
amity, but he had scarce left Palestine before he began
to form a coalition against him.   The time, it seemed to
him, was ripe.   The hot-headed Angevin might never
return.   His unscrupulous brother was a ready tool.
Even when the pope called shame upon him for his

desire to be absolved from his oath to protect Richard's dominions he was not checked. It was no time, he felt, for nice consciences. The hour had come when Normandy might be won.

Philip did not let the grass grow under his feet. A month after his return he went to the old meeting-place at the edge of the great Norman plain betwen Gisors and Trye, and demanded of the seneschal and barons of the duchy his sister Alais, then prisoner at Rouen, and the castle of Gisors with the counties of Aumâle and Eu. He produced a treaty which he said had been signed at Messina, by which Richard promised the lands; but the barons stoutly refused to surrender them, and Philip angrily answered that he would take them by force. It was an attempt, no doubt, to test the Norman feeling. He now turned to a more hopeful task. He offered John (who was already married) the hand of the wretched Alais, and promised to help to win all his brother's dominions. But Eleanor, the royal mother, who was her absent son's strongest support, with the English justiciars, forbade John to cross to Normandy. He sullenly obeyed, and the French knights at the same time refused to join in Philip's war against the crusader.

But all was changed by the news of Richard's capture. Before the end of the year Philip knew that his enemy was in the hands of the Austrian duke. John was again tempted, and in February 1193 he eagerly took investiture from Philip of all the foreign lands of his house.

The terms of their treaty were significant. Philip knew John's weakness, and put forth a claim which for audacity was unparalleled since William the Norman had freed himself from French tutelage. He claimed all Normandy on the right bank of the Seine, except Rouen itself, nearly half the land of Evreux, with the castles of Ivry, Vaudreuil, and Verneuil, and in the Angevin lands, Tours, Azai, Amboise, Loches, Mont-bazon, and Montrichard ; and he added too the demand that the Angevin fiefs in Vendôme should be transferred to his uncle, the count of Blois. Such grants would have gone near to make the French king lord of Gaul. Philip could not expect all at once to obtain them. He began therefore, like the Savoyards in later days, to take them as one eats an artichoke.

He did not at once begin the war. The Norman barons again were loyal to their duke, and the invasion was still postponed. But it was not long delayed. On April 12 Gilbert de Wascoil traitorously delivered the castles of Gisors and Neaufle-Saint-Martin into the French king's hands ; and so all the Norman march became his. He found none to oppose him, says the canon of Newburgh, whose loyal soul scorned the treachery of the men who had eaten the king's bread and now would not raise a hand in his defence ; for the sad fate of their lord had so broken the courage of his servants and weakened their trust that, like sheep having no shepherd, they either willingly yielded or fled from the face of him that pursued. When Aumâle, Eu, and many other castles had fallen into his hands he marched with his army to Rouen in May 1193. " With a mighty voice threatening destruction to all who should resist him, he commanded the city to be surrendered. But the earl of Leicester, the king's most faithful companion in the East, being aware of his coming, had just before entered the town and encouraged the citizens to fight boldly against the foe." Vainly for many days did Philip besiege the city. It had often kept out the French king, since the days when first the Northmen held it, and again the besiegers had to retire.

Meanwhile Philip corresponded with Richard in prison, and the king promised to yield all that had been won in Normandy. The treaty, if it had any force, was kept hardly more than a few days, for in the next spring began a new French raid. William, the Breton chaplain, glows with enthusiasm when he sings of the rich lands that were traversed, of the fine castles, and of the beautiful meadows by the banks of the Avre, the Seine, and the Epte. Vaudreuil and Neubourg and the city of Evreux opened their gates, and the Norman regents were glad to purchase a truce by a large money payment.

During the winter Philip had used every effort to induce the emperor to keep Richard in prison, but in vain. On March 13, 1194, the English king landed at Sandwich. Philip now saw that the inevitable conflict must be precipitated. He broke the truce, poured into Normandy, and besieged Verneuil. There he was using all the military arts of the day, erecting vast engines, discharging enormous stones, undermining the walls, and keeping a strict blockade upon the besieged, when Richard approached, and on the eve of Whitsunday (May 29, 1194) he raised the siege and retreated. "As if to remove the disgrace of a shameful retreat," says his keen English critic, " he destroyed in his perverse fury the city of Evreux, which he had before plundered ; nor did he even spare the church of S. Taurin, the most renowned in that part of the land, though when he commanded it to be burnt, not one man out of so great an army could be found to execute so wicked a command, so that he himself, as it is said, with some lost souls of those whom men call 'Ribalds,' entered the holy place and set it on fire." The tale, if it be untrue, yet shows the fear which Philip's name inspired.

William the Breton couples the retreat with a horrible tale. Evreux had been given, as a token of Philip's love, to John to hold. When he heard of his brother's return he began to fear, and secretly bringing in armed English, he slew the unsuspicious French garrison, whom he had bidden to feast with him. Sober history does not know this legend, but Evreux was recovered, and Philip fled.

Richard, however, was by no means free from danger. In the south, Aquitaine was in revolt, but help came from Navarre. Bertrand de Born again sang the exploits of his king. It was his last *chanson*. Montmirail, on the borders of Maine, was destroyed by Angevin rebels. But the king was the greatest general of his age. He held out against all attacks, and a new siege of Rouen called him again to the north. On July 4 the two kings rested at Vendôme and at Fréteval. In the night the French camp was hastily evacuated. Philip, some say, had then marched to the destruction of Evreux; others tell that a night attack of Richard caused a precipitate flight. The English king, it is at least clear, fell upon Philip's train, and captured spoils of great value, horses, plate, and coin, the letters of agreement with the rebels, even the rolls of the treasury and the

royal seal itself. To William the Breton it is plain the
scene recalls the flight of Benhadad and his Syrians
from Jerusalem : but the loss is even more serious, for
the clerks have now, he declares, no means of estimating the royal dues, new statistics are required,
all must be sought out and written anew with painful
labour.

The year closed in peace. Richard was busy in the
south, and the Norman regents made truce with Philip.
Years of negotiation and intrigue, mingled with fighting as fruitless as either, follow. They must be briefly
followed, but two points emerge from the study which
it is important to observe. Philip never entirely lost
his hold on Normandy ; he never ceased to scheme for
new acquisitions in it, piece by piece, as war or trickery
should give him the chance to take them. And a new
line of attack was afforded by the family relations
of the Angevin house. Richard was still childless.
His brother Geoffrey's widow, Constance, unequally
yoked in marriage with Ranulf, earl of Chester, whom
she would not suffer within her sight, held Brittany for
her boy Arthur. She was ready, as the Bretons had
always been, to prefer the distant overlordship of the
French king to the close and masterful suzerainty of
the Norman duke.

In 1196 Constance was entrapped and imprisoned,
but the Breton lords placed Arthur under Philip's protection. The war which followed was desultory and
ineffective, but Richard found an effectual support in
a new alliance with Raymond VI. of Toulouse, by which
the count married the king's sister, Joanna, the widowed
queen of Sicily. With the emperor too he began to

form an alliance, which caused Philip the greatest anxiety. There was every probability of a coalition against France, when Henry VI. died.

The election of his successor showed how strong was the Angevin house. An English chronicler says that while some voted for King Philip, some voted for Richard himself; but the result announced to the world was the choice of Otto of Saxony, son of Henry the Lion, and grandson of Henry II., to be emperor and king. Philip of Swabia, the late emperor's brother, put in a claim, and Philip of France supported him, but for a time Otto was unquestionably the stronger, and the Angevin house seemed more powerful than ever. When the truce ended the French king was too weak to make any success in war; but he turned to diplomacy with ready skill. His unhappy sister Alais, whose wretched fate it had been to be bandied about between the kings for twenty-five years, at last found a husband. She was sent back by Richard in 1195. In August her marriage with William, count of Ponthieu, was arranged, and the counties of Eu and Arques—no very safe possessions— were given as her dowry. In Ponthieu Philip would find the most valuable ally against Flanders and Normandy. But it was too late. Flanders, Champagne, Brittany itself, with Arthur, returned from the care of the French king, allied with Richard; and in 1198 Philip had to meet the most formidable coalition which had yet assailed him. He offered to surrender all that he had won in Normandy save Gisors, the key of the frontier. The usual winter truce followed. The acts of Philip show that December and January were spent in negotiation. In the spring the two kings met on the Seine, some miles below Vernon, and a second meeting resulted in a peace for five years.

Richard turned to castle-building. On the great rock of Andely rose the great castle which he called "Gaillard," the greatest protection to his Norman capital. Philip sought protection in new treaties. He won over Baldwin of Flanders to promise to aid him against all foes, and the archbishop of Rheims, with the bishops of Tournai, Arras, and Térouanne, undertook to coerce him, if need be, by ecclesiastical censures to perform his promise. Reginald, count of Boulogne, ever fickle, made the same promise, under similar sanction. With Flanders, Ponthieu, and Boulogne his allies, it seemed as if his northern frontiers were safe : but the alliance was of short duration, for Baldwin again turned to Richard, and a treaty between them was signed in the new castle which was building on the rock above Andely. Reginald of Boulogne followed the example, and, cries Rigord indignantly, "by the devil's instigation, spurned his homage, broke all his treaties and oaths, and attacked his liege lord, the king of the Franks." Philip was indeed in unhappy plight, and the chronicler who has long so loyally belauded him now has word of stern condemnation for the expedients to which he was driven. He recalled the Jews, taking a great bribe, and laid heavy hands upon the churches.

The autumn showed him in still greater straits. Richard marched through Normandy with knights and mercenaries, took Courcelles, and burnt the lands around. Philip made ineffectual resistance. The Vexin was harried. The land of Beauvais had before this been entered, and the bishop made captive ; and now, on the great rock which looked on Andely and on the Seine, rose, in spite of a quarrel with the archbishop of Rouen, who laid all Normandy under interdict because his land was taken without his leave, and of a shower of blood which fell on king and workmen at their task, a mighty castle, the greatest of all the military works of the age, which should declare and protect the sovereignty of the Angevin over all the border of the little realm of the Frankish king.

Even in its birth Château Gaillard seemed a doubly ominous menace to King Philip. From the jagged rock upon which it rose high above the narrow road that lay between the hill and the Seine, the hot-blooded Richard had thrown three French prisoners, in revenge for the surprise of a Welsh contingent hard by. Philip had not been outdone in barbarity; he had taken a bitter revenge. But the rock thus savagely notorious soon became a deadlier menace. "If an angel from heaven tried to make him stay his hand, he would have had no answer but a curse," said Richard, and by the summer of 1198 the castle on the rock of Andely became the "Château Gaillard," which the king called his fair daughter of a year old.

Philip watched its growth, and as one day he stood among his barons in sight of its massive strength, which dominates the Seine valley for many miles, he swore that though its walls were of iron, it should not keep him from the sovereignty of Normandy and the Angevin lands—aye, or of Aquitaine too, which one day should be his own. When Richard heard the saying he cried with a fierce oath that he was able to hold his castle were its walls of butter and not of iron or stone.

At the moment of Philip's lowest fortunes he was delivered. William the Breton breaks forth into a dramatic pæan. The weird sisters would no longer suffer a proud rebel to abuse their mercies. Atropos spoke in solemn ire to Clotho and Lachesis. The thread of his life must be snapped. Philip deserved the Fates' protection. Richard, greedy of gold and pleasure, should look no more on the sun. On April 6, 1199, he died at Chaluz. When the great limbs were stretched by his father's tomb at Fontevrault, and the lion heart was laid to rest in the great mother church of the Norman duchy, Frenchmen saw that the Angevin house had begun to fall on evil days, and that the time of their king's triumph had come. "God visited the land of France, for King Richard was no more."

From that moment King Philip's fortune turned. John, of all the Plantagenets the weakest and the worst, was accepted in Normandy and England as his brother's heir, and Philip was able to pose as the chivalrous champion of the orphan Arthur. The turbulent barons of Anjou, Maine, and Touraine flocked to the standard of the child under whose rule they could live unchecked. They unanimously chose him as their lord, and he did homage to Philip. At Tours Constance of Brittany placed her son in the French king's hands. He was sent to Paris to be brought up with the young Louis. Philip took Evreux and overran the Vexin. Eleanor, the aged mother of John, it is true, secured her own duchy of Aquitaine for her only surviving son, and John, in a sudden fit of energy, sacked and burnt Le Mans. But the real strength lay now altogether with Philip. His great vassals were still fickle. Otto of Brunswick,

now recognised by the pope as emperor-elect, was able
to give John, his uncle, some assistance. But Philip felt
strong enough to demand the surrender of the whole of
the Vexin to himself, and the hereditary lands of the
house of Anjou to Arthur, and on the refusal he set to
work to capture the lands for himself. For a time he
had a disagreement with the Bretons, and Arthur returned
to his uncle; but by the end of the year he was again
in alliance with Philip, and his mother had made a new
marriage with Almeric of Thouars, who would give her
son new strength in the Angevin lands.

Philip, however, had now greater dangers about his
path than any that John's hostility could bring. On
December 6, 1199, he was excommunicated by the
papal legate, Peter of Capua, for his adulterous union
with Agnes of Meran, and his land was laid under
interdict. A temporary peace seemed to him unavoid-
able. The two kings met on the arid plain which lies
between Gaillon and the rock whence the glittering
tower of Château Gaillard commands for miles the whole
valley of the Seine. A strange alliance was patched up
by the diplomacy of the aged Eleanor of Aquitaine.
Louis, King Philip's son, was to marry Blanche of Castile,
daughter of Alfonso VIII. and Eleanor, King John's
sister, and to the bride were to be given Evreux and the
lands Philip had won in Normandy.

This treaty was made in January 1200. Four months
later it was renewed with stipulations still more favourable to John. On May 22 Louis and Blanche were
married. Arthur did homage to John for Brittany, and
John himself was admitted as tenant for all the
Angevin lands. The alliance could hardly have been

intended to be permanent. Philip was already procuring support by treaties with his greater vassals and his lesser neighbours, such as Peter, count of Tonnerre and Auxerre, and the fickle Baldwin, count of Flanders and Hainault, who had not long before taken the town of S. Omer.

Philip had made peace with the pope : he took back his wife Ingeborgis. Thus this time, says Rigord, he escaped from the hands of the Romans. He now received John in Paris with ostentation, and with every appearance of friendship, in spite of that king's outrage in marrying Isabel of Angoulême, whose angry betrothed, Hugh of la Marche, was soon to throw himself on Philip's side in the struggle. He knew how to treat the idle voluptuary who now held the sceptre of Henry II. John was lodged in the king's own palace, and all the king's wines, says Rigord, were set before him and his men ; precious gifts too, gold, silver, and raiment, Spanish destriers, palfreys, and other rich presents did King Philip freely give to the English monarch, and so he returned well pleased to his own land.

The peace was of short duration. John was goading the barons of Poitou to fury. They appealed to Philip. He was now strong enough to try a fall with the Angevin. Agnes of Meran was dead. Her children had been legitimatised by the pope. Ingeborgis had been taken back. There was peace with Rome, and the barons were beginning to recognise the power of the throne.

On March 25, 1202, Philip ordered John to give up to Arthur all his French fiefs. The demand was met by a refusal. Then the English king was summoned to

answer the charges against him, and to make satisfaction
before his peers. Whether the phrase "peers of France"
had yet assumed anything of its later definite meaning
is very doubtful. It is unquestionable that in the
twelfth century the French king's court of peers meant
no more than the barons who attended the king's court.
Much later in Philip's reign the terms peer and baron are
found to be interchangeable. Yet already the romances
were having great influence on political theory. It is
possible that Philip had already, in imitation of the
mythical dignity of his ancestor Charlemagne, determined to form out of the large court of barons a court
of twelve peers. It is unquestionable that already a
distinction was recognised between those who were afterwards known as the Twelve Peers of France and the
other great vassals, but it is impossible to declare with
certainty that it was the "court of peers" which tried
John. Had it met, only one of the six lay "peers"—the
duke of Burgundy—could have been present. Innocent
III. later on protested against John's condemnation
because he was a king and had not been tried by his
peers, who were kings also. It was answered that it
was not as king but as count of Anjou and duke of
Aquitaine that he was tried. But this leaves the question
of the formation of the court still undecided. At least
there is no evidence that John was condemned by the
court of twelve peers.

Whatever the court, it is clear that a trial took place.
John was summoned in due form to answer the complaints
of the Poitevin barons. He pledged, after long haggling,
the castles of Boutavant and Tillières as surety for his
appearance. But he came neither by himself nor by

deputy. He saw that it was impossible to postpone a conflict; and he thought too, it is probable, that to compromise his dignity was an unwise preparation for a critical struggle.

He was sentenced, in default, to lose all the lands which he held of the French crown. This was an event of great importance in the legal history of the French monarchy. On this sentence depended their king's right to the lands which were afterwards seized. Years later, when the murder of Arthur filled the largest space in men's memories of this troubled time, and when Louis was fighting for the English crown, it was asserted that John's forfeiture was due to a sentence of the peers on the murderer of his nephew. But of such a trial there is no trace. It was now, probably on April 28, 1202, that the decisive sentence went forth from the French king's court that the disobedient vassal who had wronged his own men and those of his overlord had forfeited all his lands, and that the supreme lord, King Philip, might by law resume them into his own hands. From this moment, if the judgment of the court could be accepted, John had no legal right to his possessions. The lands of Rollo and of the demon-race of Anjou had come again into the hands of the king of Paris.

Philip lost no time in executing the sentence of his court. He took first the castles which John had pledged, Boutavant and Tillières, and then Longchamps, Mortemer, and Lyons-la-Forêt. He then besieged Radepont, whence he was driven by a sudden march of John. Thence he turned to besiege Gournay, which was stoutly defended by its lord. Here Philip showed the military skill for which he was afterwards renowned. The castle was

defended by a wide and deep moat filled from the Epte,
which made attack difficult and capture practically
impossible. The French king observed a large stagnant
pond which was protected by an embankment from over-
flowing into the moat. He broke down the wall, and the
flood of lake and river and moat swept away the villages
near, and undermined the walls of the castle. The
besieged were forced to quit the castle, and fled into the
neighbouring forest.

Arthur was present with the king at the siege, and
after the capture he was knighted, betrothed to Philip's
daughter, Mary, and invested with all the lands of the
house of Anjou. Normandy Philip retained for himself.

Arthur was now the unquestioned duke of Brittany.
His mother was dead, and the Bretons were enthusiastic
for their boy lord. Philip may well have looked forward
to uniting the Breton heritage with his own lands by
the results of the alliance and the marriage. But John's
forces were still stronger than the Bretons. Fougères
and Dol, so often captured by Henry II., fell into the
hands of his generals, and the country was harried up
to the walls of Rennes.

Arthur now marched with 200 knights to Tours, to
unite with the Angevin insurgents in an attack on Poitou.
Here he was joined by the Lusignans, hot against John,
who had robbed the head of their house of his bride.
They brought but a small force, and Arthur, it appears,
led no more than 250 knights in all. Yet he rashly
determined, by a sudden march, to capture his grand-
mother Eleanor, who was still duchess of Aquitaine in
her own right, and in whose untamed yet diplomatic
spirit lay John's chiefest strength. He advanced to

Mirebeau, on the frontier of Anjou, and was on the point of capturing the aged queen, when John as suddenly came up, surrounded and slaughtered his men, and took the young leader prisoner.

This was on August 1, 1202. A few months later Arthur, who had been first imprisoned at Falaise, was reported to have died, and it was loudly asserted that he had been slain by his uncle's hand. John, so William the Breton told in the Philippid, had taken the boy out with him alone from Rouen and rowed up the Seine, suddenly plunged a sword into his body, and then, rowing on again three miles in the dark night, thrown the body into the river. Be this legend or true record, nothing more was ever heard of Arthur.

The death of John's rival might seem to leave him undisturbed in power. In reality it was one more step towards the triumph of King Philip. The French king had never ceased his small expeditions on the frontier. He now passed from the position of a leader in petty skirmishes to that of the avenger of blood. Men declared later that the court of peers had found John guilty of murder, and sentenced him to death and forfeiture. So Louis, King Philip's son, loudly proclaimed in 1216 : but there is no evidence that any legal notice was taken of the crime which all men believed to have been committed. It was not yet indeed certain that Arthur was dead. Philip's charters for some time contain provisions for the preservation of his rights.

John's lands in Gaul were already forfeit. Philip now only pressed the more strongly to snatch them from his sway. He marched into Touraine, took Saumur, and then went on to Aquitaine. One by one the great barons came over to him and did him homage. Already lords such as Maurice de Craon had sworn fealty to him so long as Arthur was in prison, and now they hastened to become his men without demur.

Philip now set himself in earnest to the conquest of Normandy. Castle after castle fell into his hands. Vaudreuil, Conches, and the whole of the county of Evreux became his. John remained idly at Rouen. His men sent to him imploring aid. "Philip harries your land, your strongholds he captures, and their seneschals he ties to the tails of the horses and drags them to prison, and your property he uses as his own." "Let be," was all John's answer, "some day I will win all back."

But it was too late. Day by day came new recruits to Philip's camp. The few ill-organised efforts which John made to relieve besieged castles were easily repulsed. Step by step he won his way to the heart of the Norman lands. At last only Château Gaillard stood between him and the capital where John lay in dissolute repose. In September 1203 the siege began, and now for many months Philip's letters and charters are dated "from before the saucy castle."

The ruins of Château Gaillard still stand on the height that overlooks Little Andely at the point where the Seine makes a great bend, surrounding the peninsula of Bernières. From the keep, still lofty though it has lost one, if not two, of its storeys, the eye looks northward over the wooded heights and follows the white cliffs which run steeply up from the river as it sweeps round to Bernières. Below lie the narrow streets of Little Andely; north-west, in the valley, the town, in the thirteenth century walled and fortified, of Great Andely.

Where the Seine flows swiftly down past many a little
island, and fringed by woods, there rises a hill, standing
back from its right bank, which overlooks the castle.
The castle itself stands upon a sharp rock which rises
sheer from within a few yards of the river.   A bridge
now crosses the Seine to the southward of the castle.
Somewhat below it are three islands.   Across one of
these the bridge passed in the thirteenth century, and a
fort on the same island protected the way.

From the river-bank the castle which King Richard
built is impregnable.   A lake or large marsh then
separated Great from Little Andely, and protected the
fortress from any attack on that side.   Only from the
near hill, which commanded the foreworks of the castle,
could attack be made with any prospect of success.   On
this side the massiveness and complexity of the work is
stupendous.   First comes a deep trench, then a strong
fort with walls ten feet thick.   This was separate from
the main fortifications.   Here, besides the ditch, which was
more than forty feet deep, cut from the solid rock, the
walls were protected by the sharp cliffs on which they
rose.   The enclosure was large, and had not only towers
and bastions, which were suitable for dwelling-houses as
well as defensive works, but also casemates underground,
supported by lofty pillars, and a chapel and cellar added
by John in 1202.   This vast enclosure, strong though its
defences were, had the disadvantage of being commanded
by the outer fort, so that if that were taken it would
become difficult to hold against a force well provided
with military engines.   Within its walls, and protected
by a deep trench, rose the citadel.   It had seventeen
semicircular bastions, separated from each other by less

than a yard of wall. The walls themselves, though from eight to twelve feet thick, have generally only a casing of stone, often bevelled and built with considerable attention to effect, and within are of rubble. Towards the river they communicated with some outworks and a tower on the hillside, at a part where the fall was not absolutely perpendicular. Towards the south and south-east was a perpendicular counterscarp. The keep rose magnificently from this innermost enclosure, and towered above all the buildings, save perhaps the tower at the south-western limit of the fortification. Here was the king's own dwelling, and hence a view stretched over the richly cultivated plain of Bernières, the glorious sweep of the river from Gaillon and towards Rouen, and the surrounding hills, thickly timbered and shutting out the country to the north and the south-west. A grand house, thought the French chronicler, for kings' pleasure as well as their protection.

On the river the castle was defended not only by the bridge and fort, but by a double stockade, which protected the island from a force descending the stream. The Seine is broad and swift at the bend where the fortress stands, and the whole sweep is immeasurably finer than the lower waters where the chalk cliffs are left behind as the stream nears Rouen.

The siege of such a place was no military promenade. It was the most difficult task which Philip had yet undertaken. It differed not merely in degree from the constant castle-taking to which the feudal fighters of the time were habituated, for no castle in all Gaul could compare with Château Gaillard for the combination of natural and scientific defences.

From the first Philip prepared for a long siege. He marched across the plain of Bernières, having crossed probably at Gaillon, and encamped just below the castle, and opposite to Little Andely. The garrison at once destroyed the bridge between the plain and the island. Philip, however, was not to be prevented from reaching the opposite shore. He had brought great numbers of military engines, stores of wood, and barges for transport and to serve as bridges, and skilled arbalists, Jourdain, Paviot, and Renand Tatin, were among his officers. Some gallant French youths cast themselves into the stream and, heedless of the storm of arrows and stones which reached them from the island fort and from the castle itself, cut a way through the stockade large enough for the passage of boats. A flotilla of barges at once passed through and formed a bridge beyond the stockade and the island, which was immediately fortified with towers. Across this Philip led the greater part of his men to attack Little Andely. Thus the three defences— the island fort, the town of Little Andely, and Château Gaillard itself—were each cut off from all communications and supplies. Robert de Lacy, constable of Chester, was in command of the castle. It was well stocked with all sorts of provisions and amply provided with water, and the garrison were prepared for a long siege.

While Philip had been gathering his army and winning his first successes John had remained inactive. He now planned one scheme for the relief of his finest fortress. He gave William the Marshal command of three hundred knights, three thousand horse, and four thousand foot, with some mercenaries led by a southern mercenary named Lupicar, who had been infamous for

thirty years as a leader of those Brabançons who had so
often devastated the fair fields of France.   They were
to advance along the left bank of the Seine by night.
"John from his noted craft begged aid, and dared by
night what he dared not by day,"—so says the poetic
chronicler of Philip's history.   Meanwhile a flotilla of
transports was to ascend the river, stocked with provisions and guarded by warships, manned, says the
chronicler strangely, by "pirates" and by three thousand
Flemings.   This force was to break the French bridge
of boats, while William the Marshal destroyed the camp
on the plain.   Philip would thus be caught between the
strong fortifications and the marshes, without means of
escape, and by sorties from the garrisons his troops could
be cut to pieces or driven into the river.   It was a
skilful scheme.

Just before dawn the attack burst upon the camp,
some while before the flotilla ascending the winding
stream was ready to attack the stockade.   Ill was guard
kept in the camp on the plain.   The camp followers and
baser men, after copious potations, were killed like sheep
as they lay upon the ground; others, hastily aroused,
rushed to the bridge to escape to the right bank; others
swam across.   But the panic was stayed by William de
Barres and other knights, whose sharp words recalled the
cowards to their posts.   Bonfires were hastily lighted,
faggots collected and set on fire, and oil poured on the
flames, and then the assailants were discerned and
attacked.   The French emerged victorious from the
struggle, but the bridge had been broken by the crowd of
fugitives, and it needed to be repaired and strengthened.
Hardly had this been done and the French just laid

themselves down again to rest, when with the dawn came the flotilla, and the crews threw themselves against the bridge. The French arbalists manning the wooden towers which defended the bridge rained stones and arrows on the foe, and great beams, iron bars, boiling oil, and pitch were also thrown from the bridge on the boats as they approached; the banks too were soon lined with archers. The fight was long and bloody. The attacking force pressed on with dauntless courage, boats were upset, men were thrown into the water, and, says the French poet, sought burial from Thetis and funeral orations from the chorus of Nereids. As others fell dying on the boats, comrades would run and give them their last kisses. It was a startling sight to the king's chaplain as he watched it from his master's camp when the sun rose on the Seine dyed with blood.

At last an enormous beam at the end of the bridge of boats fell on two boats of the attacking force and sank them. The rest of the flotilla first paused, then turned to fly. Gaubert of Mantes, a fisherman whom William the Breton had often watched as a boy, with Louis des Galées and others, seized two slight skiffs and pursued. They captured two of the boats. Then they turned to attack the fort on the isle of Andely, which the failure of the attempt at relief had now left at their mercy. Gaubert was a fine swimmer, who could go under water a thousand paces. He swam to the island, reached the wall which girt it twice round, and breaking by sheer strength some wood from the outer palisade, set it on fire and threw it upon the wall. The wind was blowing fiercely, and in a few minutes the garrison was surrounded by a girdle of flames. Some were choked, some flung themselves into the Seine, the rest surrendered.

The island taken, Philip refortified it and rebuilt the portion of the bridge which connected it with the western bank. The village of Little Andely fell at once into his hands. The villagers sought refuge in Château Gaillard, and Philip settled new inhabitants in the place with two companies of mercenaries. After this there was a cessation of active hostilities. John made no effort to relieve his great fortress. Philip was content that the garrison, now increased by the fugitives from Little Andely, should be starved into surrender, and he turned to besiege and capture Radepont. A month later he returned to the Andelys, and set about in earnest the task of making the blockade effectual. Already all egress was impossible towards the river, Little Andely, or the marsh which separated the two Andelys from each other. Philip now established a camp on the hill overlooking the castle, and dug a deep trench from the marsh to the Seine bank, thus completely surrounding the castle on the only sides from which it had been possible to procure supplies. The trench was overlooked by seven wooden turrets, each surrounded by a moat and provided with a drawbridge. The army then settled down to winter in the trenches, and mocked the defenders as young birds who would have to fly with the coming of spring.

The blockade now began in earnest. Day by day the refugees from Little Andely were consuming the precious provisions, and Roger de Lacy saw starvation before him. He thereupon turned out 500 of the weakest, and a few days later 500 more. They were suffered to pass through the besieging lines. Beyond this Philip would not allow him to go. All that afterwards attempted to issue forth were received with showers of arrows as they approached the French entrenchments. They rushed back, but found the gates closed, and for three months they were left with no food but such herbs as they could pick up and the flesh of unclean animals thrown from the walls. Many, says William the Breton, had nothing for days but water; others found food in the most hideous ways. For three months the wretches lingered between the fortifications and the trenches, till Philip, who had for a while been absent at Gaillon, returned. As he crossed the bridge the unhappy creatures recognised him from his gallant following, and cried out for pity. Philip was touched. "God forbid," he cried, "that we should increase their suffering," and he ordered them to be given food and suffered to depart. As his chaplain stood among those who ran to the help of the starving wretches, he saw one who still clutched the dry bone of a dog, and would not give it up till he had actually bread in his mouth.

Months passed by. Philip was chiefly at Mantes and Vernon. At length, before the beginning of March, he determined to try more active measures. A vigorous attack, prepared by the making of a wooden causeway up to the first fortress, and carried out by miners, who undermined the wall, soon gave the triangular fort into the hands of the besiegers. This was on February 22, 1204. More difficult was the seizure of the next enclosure. The ditch was here so deep, and the rock upon which the walls rose so precipitous, that although the enclosure was commanded by the fort, of which the French were now in possession, its capture seemed almost impossible. The skill and daring of one man, however, gave it into Philip's hands. One Ralph, whom men called Bogis, or Snub-nose, observed a little window in the new building of John on the south-eastern wall. Taking with him a few companions, he crept down into the ditch, crossed it, and climbed the sharp ascent to the foot of the wall. Then, standing on a comrade's shoulder, he managed to scramble into the window, which was unbarred. His companions followed. They found themselves in the chapel, or—for it is impossible from the statements of the chroniclers exactly to recall the arrangement of the building, which is entirely destroyed—a store-house below it. From this they endeavoured to get into the inner court, but found themselves shut in. The besieged, hearing their cries, set fire to the building. The flames spread, and the gallant Frenchmen escaped from the ruins; while the garrison, seeing it impossible to hold the burning fortress, retired to the citadel, and Ralph Bogis let down the drawbridge for the French to enter. It was a brilliant and courageous deed, and we do not wonder to read among the king's grants that the gallant Bogis was given a knight's fee "for the service which he has rendered us."

There remained now only the citadel with its towering keep, which looked far along the valley of the Seine. Gaze as he might, Roger de Lacy saw no help coming. John had deserted him, and left the chief fortress of Normandy to its fate. Only 180 warriors remained to guard the "saucy child" of Richard. Brief was the

last attack.   A small causeway gave approach to the
main entrance.   Across this a military engine was led,
under cover of which the wall was undermined.   A
countermine only served to increase the danger.   Another engine hurled massive stones against the wall.
It fell in, and the besiegers poured through the breach.
None of the defenders would yield, but they were
overpowered.   It is a curious illustration of the character of medieval warfare that only four knights seem
to have been killed during the whole siege.

It was on March 6, 1204, that Château Gaillard fell
into Philip's hands.   Its capture was the greatest
triumph he had yet obtained, and it marked his complete victory over the house of Anjou, as the battle of
Bouvines marked his victory over all other foreign foes.
From that time there was no real resistance in Normandy.
Philip offered liberal terms to all the towns which
would yield, and they readily agreed to a year's truce.

John tried to negotiate, but it was too late.   Philip
answered that Arthur must be freed before any negotiation could begin.   Town after town yielded, when the
truce was over, at the first approach of Philip.   Even
the strong keep of Falaise, the conqueror's birthplace,
surrendered after a week's siege.   Rouen made a truce
for thirty days, but before the month was over it was
clear that John would not help, and on S. John
Baptist's Day 1204 it opened its gates.

The submission of the Norman capital was not
obtained solely by military force.   Peter de Préaux,
who was in command of the city, had received no obscure
hints that it would be worth his while to make terms
for himself with Philip.   Thus on June 1, 1204, Peter

signed the capitulation with the other knights, Robert
the mayor and the representatives of the commune;
and the same month when the surrender had been
made saw considerable grants by the French king to
Peter's kindred. Philip took similar measures to con-
ciliate other opponents. He rewarded the mayors of
each town that he captured, proved ready to confirm
all charters, and even to grant new privileges. And he
was ever ready to buy new adherents. Thus he made
large grants to win over Guerin de Glapion, whom John
had made seneschal of Normandy; and his capture of
Falaise was marked by considerable grants of land to
the mayor, André Propensée, by grants of freedom to
the burghers, and by the grant of a week's fair to the
lepers of the town on the feast of the exaltation of the
Holy Cross.

With Rouen's surrender Normandy was practically
won. Verneuil and Arques were the last to submit to
the French king. In the meantime Philip's forces had
spread over Anjou and Touraine. His mother's heritage
alone remained to John Lackland.

On April 1, 1204, Queen Eleanor, that "admirable
lady of beauty and astuteness," passed away, and
Aquitaine became forfeit like the rest of John's possessions. Philip immediately marched into Poitou. By
Easter, 1205, only Loches, Chinon, Niort, and La Rochelle
held out. A year more of indecision, rashness, hasty
attack and more rapid retreat, left John deprived of
Poitou as well as the lands of his father. Philip had
won the Poitevins by bribes as well as by the sword.
Geoffrey Martel in May 1204 made his submission, and
promised to win over the barons of Anjou and Poitou

in consideration of the king's concession; and in 1205 similar negotiations were made with the count of Eu.

Philip indeed knew how to secure as well as how to capture territory. He confiscated the lands of all those who would not abandon their former master. He introduced new settlers: he gave the government to his own men. He bound the barons together by mutual obligations as to each other's fidelity; and he never forgot to propitiate the communes and the Church. He had now truly become master of France.

John had made some efforts, not altogether successful, to recover his hold of the southern lands, but his difficulties at home, his want of money, and his quarrel with the pope made him eager for peace. Innocent, during the last year's war, had intervened in vain endeavour to check Philip's too rapid triumph and to induce both kings to enter upon a crusade. But two legates who appeared before the French monarch during the siege of Château Gaillard had been sent about their business in a manner characteristic of Philip's attitude towards Rome when he had nothing to fear from papal animosity. Now Innocent had a serious English quarrel on his hands, and the truce which was signed at Thouars on October 26, 1206, was not of his making. It was to last for two years. The time was spent by Philip in consolidating his conquests and securing his position in Europe. He took securities for the fidelity of the constable of Normandy. He made arrangements for the safe custody of the chief towns on the Loire with the seneschal of Anjou. He made terms with the irritable and vigorous archbishop of Rouen, and he confirmed the privileges of the city itself, which under

the Norman dukes had always been considerable. He
rewarded his faithful servants, such as the arbalist
Paviot, who had done yeoman service at Château
Gaillard, and his marshal Henry Clement, to whom he
gave the castle of Argentan. He took minute interest
in the affairs of Norman churches and communes. He
made frequent visits to his new possessions, and stayed
at Château Gaillard, at Gisors, and Evreux, and the
people began to be accustomed to the sight of their
sovereign. He strove too to become more closely concerned with the affairs of the outlying states, such as
Ponthieu and Boulogne. In September 1208 he ratified
a marriage alliance between those two states, and three
months later he intervened in a dispute between the
count of Ponthieu and the bishop of Amiens. The
charters of these years show a continued process of
absorption and consolidation of the new lands.

When the truce expired neither party was anxious to
resume the war. Philip had enough on his hands at
home, and the Albigensian crusade, which he watched
with such astute prudence, promised a more favourable
and less costly opportunity for enlarging his dominions
than any that a war with the English king could afford.
John meanwhile was getting deeper and deeper into the
mire, and all to the profit of the French king. His
tyranny was causing many of the barons to seek refuge
under Philip's protection. Innocent in 1212 began
to appeal to the king whom he had so long banned,
to take arms against the tyrant who was now under his
anathema. When at length the sentence of deposition
was pronounced against the English king, it was to France
that the pope looked for the execution of the sentence.

The pope's legate and the English bishops published the
sentence in France.   Already half the great men of
England lay under special sentence.   " An index excom-
municatorum," said the late Mr. Pearson of this time,
" would be very like a peerage."   English malcontents
were eager to throw themselves into the arms of France.
Llewelyn, the prince of North Wales, allied himself
with the French king.   Then King Philip, says Matthew
Paris, understanding and welcoming what he had so
long desired, girded himself to the battle, and called
all the men of his realm to meet at Rouen for the
invasion of the English lands.   He gathered too a
fleet and enormous stores of provisions.   He held a
great council at Soissons, at which his barons (save
Ferrand of Flanders, who was already in secret alliance with John) enthusiastically greeted the project
of an invasion of England under the pope's blessing.
But John was not without other help among Philip's
vassals.   Reginald of Boulogne, who had turned from
side to side since Henry II. was the English king, but
who in later years had been Philip's trusted counsellor,
and had aided him in the conquest of Normandy in 1204,
now threw himself with Flanders, and the imperial
claimant Otto, on the side of the coalition against France.
He had long been engaged in a bitter quarrel with the
bishop of Beauvais, he had strongly fortified and pro-
visioned the castle of Mortain, and only yielded to a
sudden march and imperious summons of the king.
On the principle that like will have like, the French
chroniclers readily explain Reginald's desertion.   His
little daughter was pledged in marriage to Philip
Hurepel, King Philip's son ; the contract had been signed

in November 1209. His wife was a very noble lady, and from her came the county that he held. But he was forgetful of all moral ties, a persecutor of communes, of churches, of the poor, and a man of the most profligate life. Excommunicate himself, he turned naturally to the excommunicate emperor and the excommunicate king. As early as 1211 Philip had discovered his treachery, He offered him pardon, but told him he must come to Pont de l'Arche to obtain it, under threat of the immediate seizure of Mortain, the castle given to him in 1204 in exchange for Mortemer, and the chief fortress he possessed in lower Normandy. Reginald had shuffled and promised and disobeyed, and in May 1212 he had done homage to King John.

In the early summer of 1213 Philip determined to deal with the foes on his northern border. On May 10 he arrived at Boulogne, whence he passed to Gravelines, where he had demanded the presence of Ferrand. He had already taken pledges from all the neighbouring cities and churches for their support against the coalition. Ferrand did not come, but there appeared a less agreeable visitor. Pandulph, legate of the pope, crossed from England to announce the formal submission of John to the Holy See, and the order of Innocent to the French king to cease from his expedition. Thus at the moment when he might have felt most sure of success, a certain victory was snatched from his hands. He paused in his designs against England, but he did not delay to avenge himself on Flanders. He marched thither and took Cassel, Ypres, Bruges, and Ghent. He was successful on land, but a terrible disaster befell his ships. His fleet, anchored at Swinemünde or Dam, the port of Bruges, was attacked by a fleet of 500 ships, under William Longsword, earl of Salisbury, and with the aid of the count of Boulogne was almost entirely destroyed. Philip was compelled to return to France; and the tide of invasion turned against him.

In July 1213 John prepared to go to Poitou, where the barons were as ready to rise against Philip as they had been to harass his Angevin predecessors. He was delayed by new troubles at home, but when at length a temporary peace was made he sent money to William of Salisbury and the troops in Flanders, and on February 2, 1214, himself crossed to Poitou and landed at La Rochelle, where the barons did homage and vowed their easy fealty. With the strange change of fortune which is so characteristic of these wars, he at first carried all before him. He stormed the castle of Miravent, and brought Geoffrey of Lezinan to sore straits. He won over even the count of Marche whom he had so deeply wronged. He crossed the Loire, won a battle near Nantes, took Angers, and besieged La Roche-aux-moines. Philip, already occupied in Flanders, could not himself meet this new attack. He sent his son Louis, a young warrior with all a young warrior's energy. At the news of his coming the fickle Poitevins declared that they could not dare a pitched battle, and John was obliged to retreat. Louis had himself been unwilling to engage, though he had an army of 2000 horse and 7000 foot, but when he heard of the retreat he turned to pursue. No decisive action, however, seems to have taken place, though William the Breton (who was with Philip in Flanders at the time) declares that Louis drove John back in disorder across the Loire.

John's idle procrastination and the fickleness of his barons deprived the southern war of all real interest. In the north the battle of Bouvines, July 27, 1214, made the English King thankful to agree to a cessation of hostilities. On September 18, 1214, at Chinon the two kings agreed on a truce till Easter 1220. The possessions of each were to remain as they were at the signing of the truce. John returned to England on October 19. From that day all hope of regaining the Angevin dominions in France was abandoned, and the triumph of Philip was complete.

In nothing does the great king's genius appear more clearly than in the methods he adopted for securing the heritage he had acquired. The policy of supporting the under tenants against their lord, of which the most striking instance was the trial and condemnation of John for his ill-treatment of his Poitevin vassals, was consistently followed throughout the struggle which ended in the acquisition of the Angevin dominions by France. The Norman barons, the mayors of Norman towns, received rich rewards for their desertion of their duke. In Anjou Geoffrey Martel made submission May 1204, and promised to win over the barons of that land. A year later the count of Eu received the grant of the royal domain in Poitou for five years, with an income of 4000 livres, and the service of 100 knights and 1000 men-at-arms, that he might win Poitou for the crown. The churches were propitiated by special grants of protection, and William the Breton records with delight that freedom of election was given to all the Norman sees. The barons who could not be relied upon received exchanges of their fiefs for lands lying near Paris.

Confiscated lands, of which there were many when the Norman barons had to choose between their English and foreign estates, were added to the domain of the crown or distributed among loyal barons, both small and great. The acts of the four years 1203 to 1207 contain more than fifty such grants. While the power of the old nobility of the newly-conquered lands was weakened, every opportunity was taken to raise up the towns by grants of immunity and commercial privilege. Philip knew not only how to win but how to hold.

The fall of the Angevins had been largely the result of their own suicidal dissensions and of John's vicious incapacity. But Philip had shown his greatness by his patience and his prudence. It was the slow indomitable pursuit of an end steadily set before him from the first— the persistent unceasing blows at the mighty edifice of the great King Henry—that had at last accomplished the task of the French king, and made possible the creation of an united France.

CHAPTER IV

BOUVINES

THE long struggle with the Angevin house did not occupy the whole of Philip's energies. His father had avoided, when he could, direct relations with the Empire, but by extending his influence over the ecclesiastical states on his frontiers had endeavoured to win support against the possible aggression of a strong emperor. Philip was more ambitious. Not content with securing his own safety from attack, he aspired to interfere in the internal politics of the Empire. The relations of France with Germany entered upon a new phase. But Philip was nothing if not cautious. At the beginning of his reign he was urged on the one hand by Henry II., to whose wise advice he owed so much, to support the cause of Henry the Lion of Saxony against the Emperor; on the other he was warned by his uncle the count of Champagne to avoid any active intervention. He prudently kept peace with Frederic. He had enough to do, indeed, to defend his own claims of suzerainty. When his war with Philip of Flanders was in progress, the count, who was vassal also of the emperor, had sought his aid. Frederic declared that he would protect his vassal, and the French king found his suzerainty over Flanders merely nominal when a stronger suzerain supported his vassal. In 1184, and again in 1185, the succours of the German kingdom were promised to the Flemish count against his French lord. It had seemed as if the full strength of the German kingdom would be joined to that of Philip's own great vassals against the young king; but he was preserved not only by his own skill but by the wisdom of the Emperor Frederic. Italy and the pope were enough to employ Frederic's thoughts and his power: he forbade his son to meddle with the Flemish quarrel. In the next year, with equal sagacity, he declined to support the duke of Burgundy, who was also his vassal, against the French king. He did not intend, he declared, to extend the boundaries of the Empire. He had begun in fact to perceive that Philip's hostility was dangerous. The archbishop of Köln was in alliance with him: the archbishop of Trier, banished from his see, found refuge within the French dominions. France, it seemed, would throw her weight in favour of the pope against the Empire. The emperor, however, was still too strong for the French king, and he now had Henry II. of England at his back. Philip's opposition wavered and broke down. The crusade came to distract Frederic's attention; and from 1188 the French royal house was in alliance with the Hohenstaufen. Even the friendship of Philip with Tancred, the usurper of the emperor's rights over Sicily, did not long alienate the Emperor Henry VI. from the French king. For Philip's sake he held Richard captive, and when he had released him he was still anxious by a personal interview

to make a firm alliance with France. Henry was himself
in danger ; the princes of the Empire, it seemed, needed
only French aid to make their rebellion successful. His
meeting with Philip did not take place : only three times
in the twelfth century did a Roman emperor speak face
to face with a king of the Franks. But the alliance was
made, and Philip endeavoured to confirm it by a marriage
proposal. He had repudiated Ingeborgis : he sought now
the daughter of the Count Palatine for wife. The lady
proved an unexpected obstacle to the international
arrangement ; she was already pledged to Henry of
Brunswick, the son of the Lion of Saxony, and she con-
trived to marry him in spite of her father and the
French king, and the Holy Roman Emperor. The
marriage, instead of leading to war, brought about reconciliation between the Emperor and the house of Brunswick,
and Philip found himself before long opposed by a
coalition of which the Emperor with Richard, his new
vassal, were the prominent members. Philip strained
every nerve to induce Henry to retain his rival in captivity,
but the emperor showed his proposals to Richard, and
thus definitely espoused his cause against the French
king. But Philip was again preserved from any direct
attack of the imperial forces. Henry's Sicilian conquests,
his constitutional projects and dynastic difficulties, kept
him fully employed, and when he died in 1198 Philip
no longer feared German intervention, but was able himself to take part in the quarrels of the princes of the
Empire. He threw himself at once upon the side of
the late emperor's brother, in enmity to the Brunswick
house. On June 29, 1198, he made a treaty with Philip
of Swabia, and he persistently endeavoured to induce

Innocent III. to discard Otto.   But he was a shifty ally.
Before many months were over the pope had won him
round.   He gave no support to Philip of Swabia: he
thought only of his struggle with the Angevins, and he
was pleased with the distractions of the German kingdom.
So negotiations lingered on till the murder of the Swabian
in 1208.   Two months later the French king agreed
to support the new claimant, Henry of Brabant, against
Otto.   Three years before, in February 1205, the French
king had bound the duke of Lorraine to his interest
by bestowing on him a pension of 200 marks of silver,
when the duke did homage against all others saving
his duty to Philip of Swabia, king of the Romans.
In August 1208 king and duke met at Soissons.   A
mutual alliance was promised against John and Otto.
If the count of Boulogne should oppose them, Philip
promised to make one of Henry's sons count in his stead.
Philip supplied the new candidate with 3000 marks of
silver to forward his election to the Empire.   It was
agreed that if Henry should become emperor the alliance
should be formally renewed, and that any disputes between the Empire and the kingdom should be submitted
to arbiters—two from each realm, with a fifth impartial
person added in case of need—who should meet on safe
ground between Cambrai and Péronne.   The alliance
bore no permanent fruit.   The opposition broke down,
Philip's money was thrown away, and there followed
two years of wearisome intrigue.   Some thought that
the French king himself wished to become Cæsar and
Augustus, but if he held the idea he soon abandoned
it.   In 1212 he warmly espoused the cause of the
young Frederic, the heir of the Hohenstaufen.   At

Vaucouleurs in November his son Louis met Frederic and concluded an alliance. Philip threw himself with some energy into the contest. He sent special agents to influence certain of the electors, and did not forget to place at the new candidate's disposal a sum of 20,000 marks, which we have evidence was spent.

Thus Philip had actively intervened in the internal affairs of Germany. He asserted a position which Richelieu and Louis XIV. and Napoleon were to follow up. He formed a coalition which placed Frederic on the throne, and prepared to defend him. Otto, half despairing, tried to meet his foes by joining with England and Flanders in a desperate attack upon the French dominions. This was the situation in the summer of 1214. It was the culminating point in the relations between France and Germany during the century; a supreme moment in the strife of Welf and Wiblingen, as well as in the reign of the great French king.

But the forces of Otto were not the most dangerous foes with whom Philip had to contend in the summer of 1214. Far more important was the struggle with Flanders. To understand this it is necessary to retrace our steps to the time when Philip of Flanders, the friend and adviser of Philip's youth, the "most honest and powerful" man whom Gilbert of Hainault commemorates, died at Acre.

Philip Augustus had lost no time in claiming the Flanders heritage for his son Louis. The lad's mother was daughter of Baldwin V. of Hainault and his wife Margaret, sister of the dead count of Flanders. The claim was vigorously asserted by William of Rheims and the regents, who disputed with Baldwin of Hain-

ault the allegiance of the thriving towns over which
the French king had so long sought to rule—Bruges,
Ypres, Courtrai, Alost, Oudenarde.   Ghent remained for
a while in the hands of the widowed Countess Matilda.
When King Philip came home he found his regents
successful, but Baldwin still uncrushed, and he wisely
contented himself with a division of the country such as
he declared had been promised when he wedded Count
Philip's niece in 1180.   Bapaume, Arras, Aire, S. Omer,
the strong castles of the counts of Flanders at Ruhout
near Arques, Hesdin, Lens, with the homage of Boulogne,
S. Pol, Gisnes, and Lille—this contented him, and he
left to Baldwin of Hainault the title of count of Flanders,
with all the northern part of the Flemish lands, as well
as the march of Namur which he had recently assumed.
The division was not made till Baldwin had himself
visited Paris and "found no equity or kindness in the
French king," and had returned hastily, being warned
by men of the king's household that Philip intended to
keep him prisoner.   Then Philip changed his former ill
counsel, for he saw that the Flemish towns were eager
in support of Baldwin, and met the count of Hainault
at Péronne in February 1192.   There the concord was
made and the land divided.   Baldwin did homage for
the part of Flanders which he held of France.

For a time the settlement seemed satisfactory.
Baldwin of Flanders joined the French king in his
Norman campaign of 1193.   But any signs of the
superiority of the Angevin house were eagerly accepted as
encouragements to desert the French interest.   Baldwin
died in 1194, and the new count had no love for his dead
sister's husband.   The great rising of 1197-98 gave an

opportunity which Baldwin VI. eagerly accepted ; much
of Artois was recaptured, and when Philip, rashly venturing, as the chronicler thought, where his forefathers had
not dared, attacked Flanders, he narrowly escaped capture near Ypres. When the fourth crusade started the
romantic young count of Flanders eagerly joined it.
The foundation of the Latin Empire of the East, and
his own accession to the throne, diverted Baldwin from
all the interests of Western Europe, and did much to
save Philip at a critical epoch of his life.

The struggle with the house of Anjou was more than
enough to occupy the French king in the years that
followed, and when Baldwin died and his little daughter
Jeanne was given in marriage to her kinsman Ferrand
of Portugal, the overlord did not interfere. He even
abandoned the pretensions of his son Louis to the rest
of Flanders on the cession of S. Omer and Aire by the
new count. Ferrand soon proved at least as active an
antagonist as his predecessors. He alone at Soissons, on
April 8, 1213, refused to aid Philip against John; and he
threw himself heartily into the coalition against France.
For some time he kept his definite alliance with John
and Otto ; twice he failed to keep tryst when his French
overlord summoned him. At length Philip saw that he
was too dangerous an enemy to be left on his flank while
he attacked the English king, and determined to make
a decisive attack on Flanders. He was not without
encouragement. Some of the towns, always ready to
intrigue against their rulers near at home, seemed ready
to cast off Ferrand. Tournai, both as a municipality
and as a bishopric, was for Philip. A sketch of their
past relations will throw light on the position in 1213.

The city of Tournai, which was to become an extremely important factor in the relations between the Flemish counts and the French king, occupied an unique position on the borderland. It was subject neither to Flanders nor to Hainault. Its bishop, who since 1146 had ceased to combine with that see the bishopric of Noyon, was the lord of the district, under the suzerainty of the French king, to whom he owed the service of ten knights. Ecclesiastically the bishop's authority extended over all Flanders. If he were a partisan of the Flemish counts he could do much to nullify all influence of France in the land. If he were a nominee of France he might be of the greatest service to the aims of the French kings. But the prelate's political influence was little felt within the walls of his city : the citizens paid little heed to the lordship of their bishop. They went their own way, and were their own masters. Early in his reign Philip saw both the strategical and the political importance of the city, and in 1187 he determined to visit it in person. He acted upon the advice of his father-in-law, Baldwin of Hainault, who was now eager to secure the alliance of France, to procure for his wife, on her brother's death, the succession to the Flemish fief. It seems also that a baron of Flanders holding the title of Castellan of Tournai—Everard Ralph III.—jealous of the position of the bishop, now that he was no longer occupied with the affairs of Noyon, was endeavouring to turn his honorary office into a real lordship, and to throw the power of the district on the side of Philip of Flanders. Local and family reasons appear to have made the bishop, Stephen of Avesnes, ready to welcome Philip as a deliverer from the difficulties of his position. This was Philip's opportunity. He asked, says Philip Mouskes (probably a contemporary witness), of whom the bishop held the city. "Of Our Lady and of God," said the bishop, "and of you and the kings your sires." But the citizens were unruly vassals, and he would willingly surrender all his rights into the king's own hands. Let Philip himself be the direct lord. The king eagerly accepted the offer and departed well pleased. But he had still to reckon with the citizens, and he reckoned royally. He confirmed all their previous privileges, and he granted to them exceptional rights which freed them from the castellan as well as the bishop, and gave them a constitution on lines of the completest self-government existing at that age. In return, they became pledged to send three hundred men-at-arms at his call to war. They loyally discharged their obligations. In 1197 they refused entrance to Baldwin, then count of Flanders and at war with France. They suffered for their loyalty to their new lord, and had to pay a fine of 4000 marks. Again in 1213 they suffered the horrors of a siege. But their union with France was a political fact of the highest importance. The district which became French was of the first value to the French crown. In the crisis of 1213, both as a municipality and as a bishopric, it sided with the French king. Its bishop, whose see was subject to Rheims, excommunicated Philip's foes. At length a force set out from Paris to chastise the too daring vassals of the north. But Ferrand with his allies was still more than a match for the king. When the French fleet attacked Dam it was utterly destroyed.

William Longsword and Reginald of Boulogne, with
Ferrand, beset it by sea and land, and a great number of
ships were burnt. The invasion of Flanders by sea
was thus decisively checked. On land Ferrand took
Tournai and Lille, but was driven from both. The
towns now sent him powerful aid, and it was with a
strong army that he joined Otto at Valenciennes early
in July 1214. Philip had been long watching the
Flemish frontiers, and while his son Louis was meeting
John in Anjou, he was preparing for a decisive contest
with his northern foes.

The frontiers of Flanders were defended by the
Somme and the Scheldt, and the marshes which surrounded them. Between the two rivers it was the
constant aim of the invading French armies to force a
way; and a bridge at Bouvines across the marsh by
a little stream, the Marcq, gave a passage which the
leaders naturally sought on the way to Tournai, a town,
sympathetic to France, which held the passage of the
Scheldt and the entry into Flemish territory.

Otto's army moved, between July 25 and July 27,
from Valenciennes to Tournai along the left bank of the
Scheldt. As it marched, it had on its right the swamps
round that river, on its left the great *Forêt charbon-
nière*, which in earlier times had stretched from Lille to
south of Cambrai, but which now had been separated
by small monastic settlements into several distinct
woods. Through the forests (or between marsh and
wood) there lay, to the west of the modern road, a fine
paved Roman way, which crossed the little rivulet
called the Barge before entering Tournai. Philip
approached this forest from the south-west, burning

as he went to the right and left of his march, and
"royally devastating." He passed by Péronne to
Boulant-riez at the south of the open ground which led
to Tournai. On July 25 he was at Bouvines, on the
26th he entered the fine city which his father had always
sought to befriend. Tournai to-day, with its Vauban
citadel and its magnificent earthworks, is very different
from the little city of the thirteenth century,—more
different still from the Civitas Tornacensium of earlier
days. But parts of its old walls may still be discerned, its
two famous towers stand on the bridge that guards the
Scheldt, and it is still a city of clerks and churches, as
when the Flemings who had seized it in the previous
year and had wrung from its burghers the profits of
their trade deserted it at the coming of Gerard La Truie
with 300 knights. On July 25 King Philip entered the
gates. Otto meanwhile was advancing northwards. He
was at Mortagne on the 20th, and by his spies knew all
that passed in the French camp. He hoped to blockade
the French army within the walls of Tournai, and by
the numbers of his men to force them to surrender.

In Philip's camp the gravity of the situation was
fully apprehended. While the king pondered, accusations of treachery were freely bandied about among the
barons. The count of S. Pol, whom men suspected
because King John a month before had in a special proclamation reserved his lands from all ravage, answered
Guèrin the warrior-priest with a scornful laugh, "A
good traitor will you find in me." Long the council
lasted. The French knights cried out that by a feigned
retreat Otto might be lured from the marshes into the
open. It had been Philip's aim from the beginning of

the campaign, and the idea was eagerly accepted. On
the 27th he marched from Tournai, intending, says
William the Breton, to lie the next night in the fortress
of Lille. His road along the old Roman street lay
considerably to the south of the modern way between
the two great frontier towns, and led across the plateau
of Bouvines which he had crossed two days before.

To the emperor the evacuation of Tournai seemed
clearly to be a retreat. Only Reginald of Boulogne,
who had been Philip's favourite counsellor, declared
that it was not the fashion of the French to fly. His
protests were unheeded. It was unanimously decided to
pursue and fall on the French at the passage of the
Marcq. Hugh of Boves, leader of the Brabançon
mercenaries, cried out upon Reginald as a traitor and a
coward. "The battlefield to-day," answered the count
of Boulogne, "will prove you a traitor and me a true
man." Within a few hours of when Otto's spies told
him of the French king's determination—which had
been publicly announced in Tournai for the sake of
deceiving the enemy—the allied forces were on the
march. If Otto succeeded in intercepting the French
retreat it must be before Philip crossed the Marcq—that
is, the armies must meet on the plateau of Bouvines. The
neighbourhood has undergone considerable changes since
the thirteenth century. Marshes have been drained
and forests thinned, and new roads and bridges have
been made. But the careful examination of French
archæologists and military historians, with a personal
inspection of the ground, makes it easy to discover the
site and recall the incidents as they happened.

Bouvines itself is a little village within a few miles

of the French frontier, and within 9 miles of Lille as the
crow flies, but considerably farther by road.   The village
stands on the edge of a highly-cultivated tableland just
where it slopes down to the little stream of the Marcq.
To the north of the village and of the plateau where the
battle took place are some low-lying fields on to which
in a rainy season the waters of the little stream overflow.
North-east lies the road to Tournai, and south-east of
it the prosperous village of Cysoing.   South there flows
the Marcq among water-meadows and woods.   It is a
site that seems formed by nature for a battle-ground.
In the centre of the open space there is a dip in the
ground, and near it goes the old Roman road from
Tournai, now little better than a track across the fields.
The soil is chalky, and modern draining has still left
swamps by the river bed.   Southward are copses among
which flows the Marcq, and on the north, both by the
stream and by the little village of Gruson, the ground
falls and is thickly wooded.

Early on Sunday morning July 27, when they had
heard mass, the French moved out from Tournai.
Guèrin rode southwards to reconnoitre.   A professed
brother of the Hospitallers he had been, and long the
trusted councillor of the king.   Strong in repressing the
immoral disciples of Amaury of Chartres, he was at
heart more of a knight than an ecclesiastic.   To him
Philip had already in this war given important military
commissions, and he was now to be as much the chief
general as the king himself.   As he rode southwards he
soon saw the advancing force of the allies, the infantry
in front as prepared for battle after the fashion of the
time, emerging from the marshes and cutting across to

50575

the east of Tournai to fall upon the line of the French retreat. The scheme then had succeeded, and the gallant clerk rode hastily back to tell the king. He found him ready to cross the bridge of Bouvines. Philip at once halted and took counsel. It was decided to place the baggage in safety on the other side of the Marcq, and the bridge was hastily widened so that twelve men abreast could pass over it. The king meanwhile lay down to rest under the shadow of an ash on the high ground by the Church of S. Peter, from which he could see the enemy as they advanced on to the plain of Bouvines. The new church stands on the site of the old one long since destroyed, and the present bridge is said locally to be in the same place as its predecessor, though probably it is somewhat more to the north. When he had rested and taken some food he called his household guard around him and embraced them as his brothers-in-arms, William des Barres, Matthew de Montmorency, Michael de Harnes, Gerard la Truie, Pierre Malvoisin—their names were long famous in French song. Later legend makes the king call to his barons that the worthiest might wear his crown, for each was as much king as he. Philip was far too wise thus to compromise his pretensions. Then he went back to the little church and, kneeling down before the altar, said a short prayer. The words that Mouskes, the clerk of Tournai, puts in his mouth are too characteristic to be altogether fabulous. "Lord, I am but a man, but I am king. Thine it is to guard the king. Thou wilt lose nothing thereby. Wherever Thou wouldest go I will follow Thee."

The rear-guard was already seen to be engaged with

the enemy.   A moment later the king put on his
armour, and with glad face "no less than if he had been
bidden to a wedding" leapt upon his horse.   "A tall
man upon a great steed" he rode along his ranks, and
thus he spoke: "Let us hasten to succour our companions.
God will not be wroth with us that we fight on His
holy day, for no fault was it counted to the Maccabees
that they repelled their enemies on the Sabbath.   Yea
rather does the day befit us, the friends of Him to
Whom ever on this day the whole Church makes supplica-
tion."   Then he rode forward to the front rank, "where
no man stood between him and the foe."   The advance-
guard of the enemy were driven back, and the French
troops formed up across the Roman road, their left
resting on the woody slope that protected Bouvines to
the north.   Above them on slightly rising ground lay the
allied forces facing almost due south, their right nearest
the Marcq.   They had marched in three divisions, and
so they formed themselves in battle array.   To their
right was William Longsword with his men.   Next
came the men of Oudenarde, Hugh of Boves and his
mercenaries, and Reginald of Boulogne with his knights
and footmen.   In the centre were ranged the infantry
of the Flemish towns, with behind them the horse and
foot of Brabant, and Otto with his German knights.   To
the left was Ferrand with the chivalry of Flanders.

The French right was also all cavalry.   Soissons sent
its contingent and the counts of Champagne, Montmorency, S. Pol, Beaumont, Melun, were there, and the
knights of Burgundy with duke Otto at their head.   In
the midst was the infantry of the French communes
with the king's household guards; at the left men-at-

arms and knights of the great vassals and the tenants-
in-chief. There was little more than 200 yards between
the armies, and a dead silence fell on all as Philip surveyed his foes. Opposite could be seen Otto in the
midst of a strong phalanx, with his golden eagle borne
erect on a dragon's back, in a car like the *carroccio* which
the Italian cities took with them to the field. Then
King Philip spoke to his soldiers. "Our whole trust is
in God. King Otto and his army are excommunicate by
the Lord Pope, because they are foes and destroyers of
holy Church, and the money which is their hire is won
from the tears of the poor and the robbing of the
churches and the clerks. But we are Christians and
enjoy the communion and the peace of the Church, and,
although we be sinners, yet submit we to the Church of
God and defend with all our strength the liberties of
the clergy. Wherefore we ought faithfully to trust
that God will be merciful to us sinners and give us the
victory over our enemies." Then the knights begged
their lord's blessing, and Philip with uplifted hand
prayed God's benediction on his men. Straightway the
trumpets sounded and the French threw themselves on
their foes.

From the right it was intended that the chief blow
should be struck. There Guèrin, the bishop elect, as
mighty a warrior as that Don Hieronimo who fought
with the Cid, had placed his knights, and he directed
his Soissons skirmishers at once against the Flemings.
For the moment the scheme was unsuccessful, for Ferrand
of Flanders and Reginald of Boulogne moved upon
the flanks of the infantry of the French communes.
They were checked by charges of French knights,

and the count of S. Pol, like Rupert at Edgehill, drove
back the right of his foes, scattering them in flight
till he was surrounded, and only with much hazard
could draw himself off and return. Then the Flemish
infantry penetrated the French centre till they reached
Philip himself. For a time the two kings stood face
to face, though they did not fight hand to hand.
Philip himself fought with all the impetuosity of a
young knight. He flung himself into the fray and
endeavoured to reach Otto. Beset on every side by the
enemies' foot, who tried to unhorse him with their long
pikes, he cleared a way through them, cutting down foes
to right and left, till a man-at-arms bolder than the rest
pierced the joints of his harness between the chest and
the head. The point of the pike remained fixed in the
triple thickness of the collar, and the king's efforts to
disengage himself served only to unhorse him and throw
him to the ground. He was in great risk of being
trodden to death, and the pike still remained fixed in
his armour. It was a moment of extreme danger. Galo
of Montigny lowered the royal banner of the fleurs-de-
lys and cried aloud for help. The French knights, led
by William des Barres, forced their way to his side and
protected him, and Peter Tristan leapt from his horse
and placed the king upon it. Philip remounted, laid
about him with a will, and, says his chaplain quaintly,
"those who had belaboured him learnt, by a like
chastisement, how imprudent it is to touch with profane hands the sacred person of a king."

On charged the knights of the king's household, and
Otto, who had come close to Philip when he was unhorsed,
found himself in the midst of his foes. Peter Malvoisin

seized the reins of his horse and endeavoured to drag
him from the field.   Gerard la Truie with his dagger
struck him a sharp blow on the chest, but the armour
did not yield.   Otto's gallant steed, rearing at a second
blow, received a mortal wound, but tore in its agony the
reins from Gerard's hand, and then forcing its way
through the enemy for a few paces, fell dead, rolling over
with its rider in the dust.   In a moment Gerard of
Horstmar was at his sovereign's side, and springing
from his horse, placed his master thereon.   For a
moment the pursuit was checked by the devotion of the
gallant knight, but William des Barres, pressing onwards,
seized Otto from behind, placing his hand between his
helmet and his neck and trying to drag him from his
horse.   Again the German knights closed round—Gerard
and Otto of Tecklemburg and Conrad of Dortmund and
a troop of Saxon knights—and plunged their swords
into William's horse.   It fell dead, and Otto was free
and galloped from the field.   On pressed the French
knights in hot pursuit.   The charge of William des
Barres scattered all before it, and when Otto fled the
carroccio was overturned and the imperial standard was
taken.

So after three hours' hard fighting William the Breton,
who had stood behind the king singing psalms of battle
in a voice choked with sobs, could look up from his
psalter and think the victory won.

On the left Salisbury and the mercenaries of Boves
had forced back the French and threatened the bridge.
Such a blow in the flank might have given certain
victory to the allies, but the bishop of Beauvais led a
gallant charge which retrieved the day.   As the English

and the mercenaries fled Reginald of Boulogne stood
sullenly aloof.   From this point the fight became a series
of scattered cavalry charges, and of brilliant deeds by
individual knights.   The allied attacks once repulsed,
the French horsemen had free space to charge, and on
centre and left and right again and again they hurled
themselves on their foes, breaking them more and more
into confusion, till at length the knights of Champagne
and Burgundy and S. Pol forced the imperial left back on
their centre, cutting them off from Tournai, and leaving
them only the woods and marshes of Willems on which to
fall back. Cramped and unable to manoeuvre with freedom,
harassed by repeated cavalry charges, deserted by their
leader and disunited among themselves, the allied forces
at last began to retreat.   First went the Flemish infantry,
then the mercenaries and the English—Salisbury had
been captured—while the German knights without their
lord still gallantly covered the retiring host.   Reginald
of Boulogne stood stubbornly on the field.   A traitor
before to Philip, he had seemed a traitor to his new allies.
He now fought stoutly to the last.   His square of
infantry could not be taken.   He extricated himself
from a crowd of Franks to throw himself against Philip
in person.   His horse was killed under him, and at last
he gave up his sword to Guèrin, the bishop elect of
Senlis.   With his surrender the battle ceased.   It was
nightfall, and the victorious army was not strong enough
to pursue.   The day ended with the completest victory
which ever befell the arms of Philip the Conqueror.
Many gallant foes had fallen into French hands, and
among them the three chiefs who had led most men to
the field, Reginald, count of Boulogne, Ferrand of

Portugal, count of Flanders, and William Longsword, earl of Salisbury. It was indeed a great victory.

The battle of Bouvines was perhaps the most important engagement ever fought on French soil. Certainly till the time of Napoleon no great French victory struck with more startling emphasis upon the politics of Europe. From the first the far-reaching consequences of the encounter were recognised. The chroniclers of the conqueror delighted to detail its incidents and enlarge upon the triumph. William the Breton indeed devotes more than three books of his poem to the campaign and its consequences. Matthew Paris, too, shows no desire to blink the importance of the English defeat; and the battle of Bouvines thus becomes almost the sole defeat of English troops of which an adequate conception can be formed from the works of an English writer. On the other hand, the Flemish and German chroniclers are significantly meagre. If Bouvines could not be minimised, perhaps it might be forgotten.

On no battle in medieval history has more diligent investigation been expended by modern writers, and we are able as a result to form a clear conception of its chief features, if we are still uncertain as to a few of the details. Of the amount of troops engaged it is not difficult to judge. The French writers, notably William the Breton, have a natural tendency to magnify the odds against which their king had to contend, but we have too many sources to be in much doubt when we attempt to form a correct estimate. It has been thought that over 6000 mounted troops were under the earl of Salisbury's command, and that the footmen were near 25,000, but the estimate is certainly greatly exaggerated. The Flemish contingent was larger. It seems barely possible that Ferrand led as many as 45,500 men to the field, of whom 40,000 were foot-men, but most probable that his forces did not exceed 25,000. Otto's force was much less powerful. He had but little command over Germany. His quarrel with Innocent III. and the skilful negotiations of the French king with the German princes had left him few sup-porters. The Brabanters and three of the Rhenish princes gave him aid, but it was neither sincere nor large. He had at the utmost 11,000 men in his force. This is a French estimate, and it is a very large one.

Philip's numbers were far inferior. He was unable to throw his whole strength into the campaign in the north. Already he had sent the greater part of his knights to join his son in Poitou, and for himself no more than 500 remained. With the squires and the mounted vassals there were probably 5000 cavalry. The communes, royal and baronial, mustered bravely, and some light-armed foot-men came with their feudal lords. Yet allowing for the tendency of the chroniclers to under-estimate the conquering force, it seems unlikely that the king had on the whole more than 25,000 men under his command, though at least one modern writer estimates the infantry at 50,000. The numerical ad-vantage was unquestionably enormously in favour of the allies, but they can hardly have been three times as many as the French. The physical features of the battlefield forbid the supposition. Natural obstacles limited the ground in the thirteenth century as they do to-day. It is difficult to think that 100,000 men could meet on the fields between Cysoing and the Marcq.

The causes of the French victory are not far to seek. Philip's army was compact, homogeneous, united. Guèrin was a born general, and the king himself could inspire enthusiasm. Fighting in the open the French cavalry had free play, and the masterly tactics of Guèrin on the right were almost inevitably successful. The allies owned no one leader, they suspected treachery, and they suffered from their very numbers. It was a great victory, and one which the skill and courage of the victors fully deserved.

Philip slept the night at Bouvines; next day he rested at Douai, and thence he began a triumphal march to Paris. The way was one continued triumph. Churches rang bells and sang Te Deum: citizens decorated their houses and thronged the streets: rustics left the harvest-fields to see King Philip ride by with Count Ferrand in chains. At Paris the whole city and the scholars of the university turned out, and the clergy welcomed the conquerors with hymns and canticles. For seven nights the city was illuminated with innumerable lights, there was high feasting and revelry, and the scholars most of all were unwearied in their mirth.

From that moment Philip's power in Gaul was uncontested. Otto retired into obscurity. The eagle which he had borne was carried from the field by the victors, and sent by Philip to Frederic of Hohenstaufen, who was henceforth undisputed emperor. Ferrand and Reginald were held long in prison. John gave up the contest. The Poitevins submitted; and the English claims from that time ceased to trouble the French king. The Church, the barons, even the young communes in their weakness, had rallied round the

oriflamme of S. Denys and the banner of the fleurs-
de-lys. It was the great day of Philip's life, the climax
of his reign of struggle and intrigue. Flanders lay at
his feet, and he was master of Normandy, Touraine,
Anjou, Maine, and Poitou.

Philip used his victory mercifully. Of him, as of
the great king Henry whom he had overthrown, the
chroniclers loved to say that he knew how

Parcere subjectis et debellare superbos.

He took no life, as he might well have done, for the
treachery which had brought him into such great
danger. Ferrand he would have released, but the
independent Flemish cities would not consent to terms
which would have made the French king safe against
their attacks. Valenciennes would not yield, and Ferrand remained a prisoner. Reginald of Boulogne was
too confirmed a traitor to be let loose. But Philip
showed a clemency rare among his contemporaries and
rarer still among his successors.

He regarded the victory over so great a force as a
special mercy of God, and a new-founded abbey, richly
endowed, rose to mark his gratitude and the greatness
of his triumph. On the edge of the forest which
lay to the south of Senlis, scarcely two miles from the
great walls behind whose solid Roman masonry the
Frankish kings had often sought refuge, and which had
in Philip's own day successfully resisted the Flemish
attack when the whole country around had been harried,
rose the great abbey of Notre Dame de la Victoire.
The gentle stream of the Nonette flowed past its walls,
and southwards it was sheltered by the forest of

Ermenonville, through which narrow bridle paths led to
Paris.   The magnificent arches of the nave still stand,
overgrown with creepers, in the beautiful garden of a
country house.   One tower rises above the broken walls.
From it the eye wanders over long tracks of woodland.
To the north the great forest of Hallate, to the south
and west Ermenonville and Chantilly, and eastwards
the rising ground which leads to the distant forest of
Compiègne.   But most prominent in the landscape are
the two towers of the great cathedral of Senlis, the grace-
ful pierced spire of the one over-topping its incomplete
fellow, but both standing vast and commanding against
the sky on the hill which the great Roman walls protected.   When Philip vowed to build his new abbey in
honour of his victory the great cathedral had been
completed but thirty years, and the castle of the old
Frankish kings, built upon the Roman walls, stood to
overawe the town.   The castle has passed away, and
the abbaye de la Victoire is a ruin, but the cathedral
endures majestic amid the fragments of lesser churches ;
and in the work of William the Breton, the canon
whose stall was in its choir, remains the imperishable
record of the day of Bouvines.

CHAPTER V

THE ADVANCE OF THE MONARCHY

WHILE Philip was winning the title of Conqueror by the success of his arms, he was achieving still more permanent victories for the monarchy by his steady and persistent attitude towards the constitutional forces by which it was surrounded. During his reign the monarchy of the Frankish kings consolidated its powers, strengthened its foundations, and looked round as a sovereign rather than as an equal upon the feudalism which had so long been dominant.

Philip Augustus and his successors were no longer the slaves of the Church, the unequal combatants of the baronial hierarchy or the vacillating oppressors of popular freedom. Philip set himself the aim of being master in his own land, and thereby the ruler of the wider Gaul. The hereditary alliance of his house with the Church was not forgotten. To that estate the Capets owed their crown, and the traditional amity implied protection of the weak, which was repaid by the sanctions of ecclesiastical discipline and censure, as important to the Crown as was the Crown's material assistance to the Church. The kings had long shielded the churches, where they could, against the wild raids of freebooting barons. The Church had thrown over the Crown the protection of holy guardianship. Philip would be the last man to break such an alliance. He saw its value, and he himself experienced its benefits. But he was claiming, more clearly than his predecessors had done, to be master in his own realm. He could stand for years in a long defiance, if not with ultimate success, against the spiritual ruler of Europe. He was not likely to be content with an attitude less firm towards the French bishops.

The protection which his predecessors extended towards Church lands, dwelt on lovingly by the chroniclers as discharged to the full by Philip, was drawn in his time into a real and direct overlordship. In his hand the *regale*, the right to the revenues of vacant sees, was exercised without restraint through nearly the whole of northern and central Gaul, and in the lands he conquered from the house of Anjou. Some of the greater vassals had disputed with their sovereigns this valuable privilege. Philip would not suffer such encroachments. His court solemnly held inquest on the claim of the vidame of Châlons to hold the see on the death of its bishop and declared against him, thus interfering outside the immediate royal domain in a manner significant of future policy. So in elections to vacant sees Philip's word was law. His most useful clerks became bishops at his will. He could, like his English contemporaries, reward state services with ecclesiastical preferment. The Church remained to him, as she had been to his fathers, the strongest supporter. From her coffers he drew gold whenever

he had need. Even her courts did not stand outside
his rule. No dispute such as rent England under
Henry II. ever disturbed the kingdom of Philip
Augustus, but an Ordinance or Establishment, issued
about 1220, is not an unfit parallel to the Constitutions
of Clarendon. King and barons, it is declared, drew
up the ordinance for the treatment of clerks. The
Church agreed that her tribunals, permitted by agreement of king and barons to deal with charges of perjury,
should abstain from all interference with feudal matters.
The jurisdiction over questions of morals remained to
the Church courts, but the lord retained his control
over the fiefs. The French clergy had claimed that
degradation should be the sole punishment of a crimin-
ous clerk. To this Philip replied in the ordinance, that
the ecclesiastical jurisdiction should not be obliged to
deliver to the civil courts the offender whom the Church
courts degraded, but that if he should be released by
the Church the king might seize him. Detention in
Church prisons was more common, it would appear, on
the Continent than in England. From judicial matters
the ordinance passed to questions of land tenure. No
burgher or villein may give to his son, being a clerk,
more than half his land; and for all he receives the
clerk must do service to his lord, and in like manner
must he serve if he should buy land. The property
given to him he may not bequeath; it reverts on his
death to the nearest kin, the clerk being allowed only
a life interest. Thus a clerk holding land is made
to hold it as a layman holds. On the other hand,
clerks were not liable to tallage in towns unless they
engaged in trade — a reasonable recognition of the

purely spiritual work among the citizens which might
be supported from the private property of the clergy. In
disputes concerning land between a clerk and a layman
the French ordinance decided after the manner of the
Constitutions of Clarendon, that first decision should
be given as to the tenure by which the land was held,
and then the suit as to the possession should be heard
in clerical or lay court according to the nature of the
fief.   A third subject is that of excommunications.
Similar to the English constitutions are the de-
clarations that no man is to be excommunicate through
a fault of his servant, or his land laid under interdict
unless his lord agrees, nor is one cited before a Church
court to be compelled by the judge to stand to its
judgment.   Most striking of all, as a proof of the power
of the French king and the almost subservient attitude
of the Pope, is the order that no man shall be excommunicated unless the lord of the fee has been asked
for his consent and has agreed.   An instance of Philip's
appreciation of the importance of commercial interests
is the order that prelates are not to impose on the
burghers the oath against usury.   It is an early recognition of the necessity of a class of money-lenders among
Christians ; and a further clause forbidding the excommunication of those who trade on Sundays or with the
Jews looks the same way.

The document is of great importance.   It is a
veritable concordat between Pope, king, and barons.
It illustrates the very different development of the
law of Church and State in England and in France.
It shows, by a marked and significant example, the
varying nature of the Pope's relations with European

sovereigns. What was banned in England was permitted in Gaul, and more indeed was conceded to Philip
Augustus than Henry the Angevin had ever thought
to ask. Popes, it is true, had changed, and the times
had changed too. But the explanation is more reason-
ably to be found in the difference between the kings.
Very different from Henry II. in 1164, in 1220 Philip
Augustus was at peace with the Papacy, and bore the
renown of a conqueror and the character of a pious
supporter of the Church. During his long reign his
unsparing exercise of the power of the *regale*, and his
insistence on his sanction to the election of many
bishops and abbats, had raised around him a clerical
hierarchy that was subservient to his will. Year by
year bishops had been chosen at his nomination. Year
by year abbeys had sought licence to elect, and had
received with the permission an intimation of the royal
will. In these last years of his reign this power was
exercised to the full. Bishops, especially those on the
outskirts of his domain, eagerly placed themselves under
his protection. The bishop of Limoges did homage in
1204, and his see was received into the king's direct
domain. In 1211 the bishop of Cahors was admitted
to the same protection. And the bishop of Clermont
in Auvergne received several grants to attach him to
Philip's interests as a political ally.

All through his reign, following the policy so steadily
pursued by his grandfather, Philip had intervened to
protect the churches from the depredations of the
barons. Rigord recounts again and again with pious
gratitude the acts of valour by which the Church was
protected and the nobles were crushed. Hebo VI. of

Charenton "began to play the tyrant" against the clergy of the diocese of Bourges in 1180 : the king heard their cries, and laying waste his land with fire and sword, compelled him to swear to give full satisfaction. It was Philip's first war.   He was only fifteen years old, but it was soon followed by another of a like aim. Humbert III. of Beaujeu, William II., count of Châlon, Gerald, count of Vienne, who had plundered the great house of Cluny and the church of Mâcon, were suppressed with a strong arm.   North and south, against great vassals and petty lords, he moved swiftly and with success.   What was begun by warlike measures was confirmed by legal arrangements.   Philip made it his aim to place monastic houses in all parts of Gaul under his immediate rule, by grants of special protection, which substituted the Crown for the lay *advocates* who had protected the great houses so largely to their own profit.   The consistent policy of many years reached its climax in 1221, when the king took under his special charge all the religious houses of the Cistercians, from Pontigny and Clairvaux down to the smallest of the cells which depended on them.

The policy thus pressed in all practical ways was enforced, wherever it was possible, by the rules of military and civil law.   The feudal service of knights was exacted from the bishops, and the persistent efforts of the rising body of legists were directed to reduce the area of ecclesiastical jurisdiction.   It was by means such as these, by protection and by encroachment, by open assertion of authority and by diplomatic extension of claims, that Philip, in spite of his long warfare with a great Pope, had for the most part the French

Church at his feet.   The estate which had raised Hugh
Capet to the throne was now almost a slave in the
hands of the greatest of his successors.

Opposed in every aspect to the Church stood the
incoherent but dangerous mass of the feudal baronage.
With the lesser lords around Paris, and with the semi-
independent barons on the frontiers of the royal domain,
the last century of the French monarchy had seen a perpetual conflict.   Philip, it might be thought, after the
work of his mighty grandfather and the persistent
diplomacy of his father, would be at his accession
master within his own domains.   Outside it, in regard
to the great fiefs, in the relations of king and vassals,
there was chaos but little relieved by almost con-
tinuous war.   Again and again the great vassals turned
against him.   At every crisis of his reign he found foes
among his chief feudatories as well as in his own
household.   We have already traced the changes in
his relations with the great Flemish fief.   With Burgundy he gradually succeeded in forming a firm alliance, for the relations between a suzerain and so great
a fief resembled far more those of two sovereigns than
the mutual obligations of feudal tenant and lord.   Hugh
III., the great Burgundian duke, began by feeling the
hand of the young king when he oppressed the churches.
The rich Burgundian land, of whose fine castles and
whose mighty river William the Breton speaks with awe,
while he does not forget the glory of its rich vines, soon
saw the invading force of the overlord.   Philip struck
right at the centre of the resistance which duke Hugh
was planning, marched towards his new castle of
Châtillon - sur - Seine, and after a three weeks' siege

captured it and reduced the duke to submission. He restored all that he had robbed from the churches, and from that moment became the king's loyal friend. Two years later he took the cross. He was with the king at Messina, and when Philip returned from the war he left to the great duke the charge of the French troops. At Acre he died in July 1192. His son Odo, who had been taken prisoner at Châtillon in 1186, remained through life the loyal friend of his overlord. In 1208 he took service against the Albigenses. In 1213 he took part in the great council at Soissons, when Philip prepared to fight his foes when he had finally distinguished the traitors from the friends. In the campaign that followed he played a prominent part. At Dam he was a leader in the pursuit, at Bouvines he fought in the thickest of the fray, and had a horse killed under him. In 1218 he died. He is commemorated, with a long list of his lands and honours, in the tenth book of the Philippid. While danger pressed from the Angevins, or when the Pope threatened the very foundation of the monarchy, the Burgundian dukes could always be relied upon to support their king.

With Champagne the king's alliance was primarily dynastic. His mother, Alice of Champagne, could call to his aid her brothers, Henry, count of Champagne, Thibault, count of Blois and Chartres, Stephen, count of Sancerre, and William, archbishop of Rheims. In the earlier part of the reign, it is true, he found them but fickle allies; but from the death of Count Henry he was able to rely on the support of the house. Thibault had entered into a new and special alliance with his suzerain, which continued till his death in 1201.

His widow Blanche was guardian for the posthumous son, Thibault IV., and did homage for his fief, remaining under Philip's especial protection. The daughters of the late Count Henry (whose mother's marriage was bigamous, being contracted after a divorce which was unrecognised by the Papacy and without dispensation) laid claim to Champagne, and the minority of Thibault IV. gave a double unsettlement. Philip was always allied with Blanche, and when at length the claim was brought to a legal decision the barons established her right and that of her son. The minority was an occasion for the exercise of enlarged powers on the part of the sovereign; but Champagne was by no means yet fully subject to the French overlord.

Of the other great fiefs the house of Anjou held two, till Philip tore them from their grasp, and Toulouse, without Philip's active intervention, gradually broke up under the long struggle between North and South which was called the crusade against the Albigenses. Vermandois and Artois were kept largely under direct royal control. Brittany, when the king obtained sway over it, was given to Pierre Mauclerc, son of Robert of Dreux and Alice, the half sister of Arthur, and daughter of Constance, the heiress of the old line. The fealty due to Philip was expressly reserved when the new Breton duke took oath from his vassals. Thus, gradually, by good fortune as well as by policy, Philip drew the great feudatories in alliance round his throne.

The great king's policy towards the lesser barons was elaborate and systematic. His own direct tenants he controlled by force and craft in turns, and above all

by the increasing influence of his judicial power. The
tenants of other lords he endeavoured in every possible
way to lure into alliance, by supporting them against
their overlords, by granting them special privileges, and
by claiming to hear their suits against their lords in his
curia as a court of appeal. Thus during all his contests
with the Angevin house Philip had allies among their
vassals. At the very beginning of the struggle his
success had come from the support of the barons of
Anjou and the southern lands, who were eager to break
from the control of Henry II. He never began a new
campaign without forming alliances that might support
him at each step into his enemies' country. The barons
of the Vexin were ever ready to pledge their friendship
with the French king against the Norman duke; and on
the north, towards Flanders, and even in the far distant
Aquitaine, there were barons eager to call themselves
allies or vassals of the lord of Paris. Instances have
been collected from Philip's acts that show how far-
reaching and systematic was this provision. In the
autumn of 1211 the vidame of Pecquigny, Thomas of S.
Valery, and Reginald of Amiens, pledged themselves his
friends against John, Otto, and Reginald of Boulogne.
All along the border, treaties were made by which castles
were held at the king's will, under pledges of the nobles
of the districts, to be returned to him at his demand.
Ivry, Avrilly, Beausart, Montrésor, Argenton, Cours,
Guarplic, Palluau, Marcheville, Lavardin, Chantocé,
Sulli, Chantecocq, S. Rémi-des-plains, Fresnay, Montrichard, Beaumont, S. Suzanne, Aigremont, Dreux—
there are many instances. Agreements were made by
which the nobles of a district were bound together in

support of the king : thus greater and lesser vassals restrained each other in the king's service.

Side by side with these politic engagements in founding the wide power of the Frank monarchy were the silent encroachments of the local administration of the Crown. Philip's predecessors, in face of the development of feudalism, had been obliged to reconstruct the administration from the foundation. The old local officials of the Karlings, who are seen still to survive under Hugh Capet, are replaced at the beginning of the eleventh century by one sole officer, the *prévôt*.

The *prévôts* were the local representatives of the monarchy throughout the royal domain, within or without the compact territory which surrounded Paris, and in the towns whose constitutions were due to royal grant. They united in their own person all the powers of the judge, the financial official, and the political administrator. Under them were the *viguiers* (vicars) and bedells, and in towns the mayors also acted at times as royal officers. As in England the sheriffs, so in France the local officials, endowed with vast powers to be used in the royal service, first enforced their authority and that of the Crown over the owners of the soil, and then, grown great by the sway they had wielded, came into conflict with the Crown itself. In the twelfth and thirteenth centuries the kings had to call to their assistance a central administration to repress the independence of their local agents. *Prévôts*, vicars, and *châtelains* (those placed in charge of strong castles belonging to the king), and the *vicomtes*, formerly the deputies of the counts, but now mostly hereditary officials themselves, bore the royal authority in different degrees, and exercised it on occasion for

their own advancement. The *prévôts*, in the feudal-
ising process which had brought the other officials
within the hierarchy of fiefs, remained, as we have
said, practically the only officials on whom the Crown
could rely. The system of administration was constantly
extended through their action, and by the time of
Philip Augustus a conflict had ensued between the
local lords, and especially the abbats and bishops, and
the local administration. Under these circumstances it
was clear that the system needed revision, and thus
before his departure on crusade, Philip instituted the
baillis, superiors in rank to the *prévôts*, and charged with
the duty of holding assizes every month to dispense
justice in the king's name, and of reporting at Paris concerning the *prévôts*, and presenting the sums collected
by them for the royal treasury. The *baillis* were to be
assisted during the king's absence by four good men of
each district, by whose advice and consent they were
to act. With their agreement the *baillis* might remove
the *prévôts* for any gross crime, such as murder or
treason; on lesser offences the king's will should be
taken. This important revision of the local administration was decided upon in the king's Council, and its
authoritative promulgation formed part of the ordinance
by which the regency of queen Alice and archbishop
William was created and its powers defined. It was a
further step towards the growing centralisation which
marked the advance of the French monarchy towards
absolute power.

In France, as in England, the closest link between
local and central administration was found in the
king's financial necessities and claims. The first duty

of the *prévôts* was to collect the royal revenue, the first duty of the *baillis* to see that it was honestly collected. Here, as so universally in medieval times, the local officials had become tax-farmers. The sums due from mills, presses, bakers' ovens, market dues, trades payments, and the actual produce or rent of land and water belonging to the Crown; for these the *prévôts* paid a lump sum, from which were deducted the expenses of repair, of fortifications and bridges, and the necessary payment for castle guard. Deductions were also made for Church endowments, for the salaries of chaplains, and for alms to churches and lepers, and for the royal huntsmen and wolf-slayers. From 1190 the *prévôts* paid little, if anything, of which they were obliged to furnish direct account; the dues which were not farmed passed through the hands of the *baillis*. To them came all payments in kind, tallages, feudal dues, town payments in consideration of charters, the profits of licences for coining money, dues from Jews, and the fines of the courts of justice. Thrice a year the accounts were presented at the treasury, and thus the central administration had ultimate control even of the great barons whom the king had made his bailiffs.

Side by side with the financial duties of the local administration, and intimately connected with them, were their judicial powers. Criminal cases came before them, and all suits concerning breach of contract, debts of Jews, and the like. Here, whatever might be the barbarous punishments in some criminal trials, the fines and profits were what chiefly concerned the king and his officials. Crime could be generally, if not always, atoned for by money payment; the king was not eager, when he judged an offender, merely, in the quaint phrase of the English law, "to betake himself to his limbs." The acts of Philip contain a number of proofs of the wide judicial competence of the *baillis*, and not a few are concerned with suits that have a financial aspect. Nor were the cases simply civil suits; ecclesiastical cases were frequently brought before the *baillis*.

In the south seneschals performed the duties discharged in the north by the *baillis*. As the lands of the Angevins fell into Philip's hands he appointed a seneschal of Poitou, making the office hereditary in the ancient family of Thouars, and a seneschal of Anjou, William des Roches, who served him well for the eighteen years following 1204; and in Normandy for a time he adopted a similar plan. Here he was reversing the policy which he had carried out in his own domain. He was giving to great local lords authority to exercise in his name, while the *prévôts* and *baillis* were men more under his own control. But so long as an astute sovereign sat on the throne, both forms of administration proved successful. The lands that Philip had won he held in peace; and the revenues of the crown were nearly doubled during his reign. In his local organisation Philip found one of the greatest material supports of his power. As Philip revised the local, so he strengthened the central administration. Under his ancestors, those who served the king in his household had been entrusted with the exercise of political power. Under Philip these officers became more and more official ministers of the crown and less its personal servants. Thus the central administration was in the hands of the chancellor, seneschal, butler, chamberlain,

and constable.   These officials acted often without much
distinction of function.   The seneschal and chamberlain
alike had commanded armies, and within the household
there was not much to distinguish the duties of the
butler from those of the seneschal or *dapifer*.   But so
far as their work may be separated, it may be said that
the seneschal was the most important.   His powers
were perhaps inherited from those of the Merwing
mayor of the palace.   He was leader of the king's
household guard, and commanded the royal armies
when the king himself was not present.   He had wide
judicial powers and a number of special privileges in
regard to particular communes and rural districts.   It
was asserted later that the counts of Anjou were
hereditary seneschals, and the statement was accepted
by many English writers, and has been repeated by
recent historians.   It is, however, without foundation.
The seneschalship, like other great offices, tended to
become a hereditary fief.   Louis VII. had struggled,
at length successfully, against the arrogant family of
Garlande.   He had then appointed a great vassal,
Rudolf of Vermandois, and Philip Augustus at his
coronation found the office held by his uncle, Thibault
V., count of Blois.   Till his death in 1191 Thibault
held the post—Thibault the "pious and merciful
seneschal," Rigord calls him.   He had taken an active
part in politics for nearly forty years when his young
nephew became king.   A politician, a warrior, a
crusader, and the holder of a vast fief, his personal
power made his official position dangerous to the crown,
and Philip never filled up the post after his death.
The recurrence of the phrase *dapifero nullo* in the

charters of the rest of the reign seems to imply that
the office was not definitely suppressed ; but there was
never again a seneschal till the fourteenth century.

Next to the seneschal stands the butler. His duties
had become more and more formal. He was administrator of the vineyards in the royal domain, but, strange
to say, William the Breton says nothing of Guy of
Senlis who held the office in his days.   The same
family had enjoyed the post for nearly a century.   In
1179 Guy, the third of the name, held the office.   In
1187 it was transferred to Guy the fourth, who remained
butler till his death in 1221.   For the last years of the
reign the office was vacant.   Like the butler, the
chamberlain steadily declined in importance.   He was
treasurer and keeper of the archives, as under the
Merwings.   Reginald, the holder of the office when
Philip became king, seems to have had no important
work to do. A year later Matthew, count of Beaumont sur Oise, was appointed.   The post had now
become little more than honorary—the duties of personal
attendance being discharged largely by deputies, of
whom we know the names of Walter de Capella, and his
sons Urso and Walter.   When Matthew of Beaumont
died in 1208, he was succeeded by one of Philip's special
servants and friends, Bartholomew de Roie, who had
served the king in the closest association for many
years, and had been prominent in the negotiations with
the Angevins and the Flemish lords.   He stood by the
king's side at Bouvines ; "a prudent man," says the
Breton, "and one specially watching for his master's
safety."   The office was now, no doubt, rather a dignity
than a definite employment.   The sub-chamberlains

were men of importance, and were employed in the most delicate and serious business of the reign.

The constable, the old master of the horse, was an official whose powers fluctuated with those of the seneschal. In 1179 Ralph, count of Clermont in the Beauvaisis, was constable. He died in 1191 during the siege of Acre. For two years the office was vacant. Then Drogo de Mello became constable, a knight of fame, who also served on the crusade. In 1218 he was succeeded by Matthew of Montmorency, who held land in the immediate neighbourhood of Paris, and survived till the days of S. Louis. Like the chamberlain, the constable was not called upon for the discharge of very active or constant duty. He was assisted in his military authority by several marshals, some of whom were prominent men and intimately associated with the sovereign. Last of all, but by no means least important, among the official signatories of the charters we find the chancellor. As in England, the chancellor was chief of the royal clerks, who served the royal chapel, conducted the king's correspondence, and issued his charters. As in England, the chancellor stood *secundus post regem in regno*, the seneschal in France being in many ways the counterpart of the English justiciar. Just before the coronation of Philip, Hugh de Puiset, son of the great bishop and earl-palatine of Durham, whose name figures so prominently in northern history during the reigns of Henry II. and his sons, was made chancellor. A second Hugh, not a kinsman, seems to have succeeded him and died in 1185. From that date the office remained unfilled, the phrase *vacante cancellaria* frequently occurring in the charters.

The work of the clerks seems now to have been directed
by two prominent men, Walter of Nemours and the
famous brother Guèrin. The former was son of Walter,
the under chamberlain, and fought by the king in the
thick of the fray at Bouvines. He, when the French rolls
were lost in the flight from Freteval in 1194, was charged
with the difficult task of replacing the lost records. By
natural skill and sound sense, says William the Breton,
he accomplished the task without difficulty. Even more
important was the great hero and churchman, brother
Guèrin. A brother of the Hospital, he became from a
clerk of the chancery the chief counsellor of the king.
During all the great campaign against the allies, it was
his military genius almost beyond question that gave
success to the French king. The "prudence and incom-
parable vigour of his counsel," which William the Breton
commemorates, made him the king's most intimate friend
(*regis specialis amicus*). He was rewarded in 1213
with the bishopric of Senlis, whose great cathedral
watches over the wooded plains where the king was often
a-hunting and where he planted the beautiful Abbey of
Victory beside the gentle streams of the Nouette.
Chancellor in name he never became till Louis VIII.
held his father's sceptre, but all through the later years
he was at Philip's right hand, and *secundus a rege* is
the title which William of Breton gives him, using
the well-known designation of the chancellor. That
one so greatly trusted and loved should never have held
the formal title shows how clear was the policy of his
master to suppress the two great offices of chancellor
and seneschal, whose official prerogatives seemed to
threaten the sovereignty of the crown itself.

By his treatment of the five great offices Philip advanced another step towards the absolutism of his grandson. Recognising that the great officials in the household, after being made the chiefs of the central administration and holding their posts as hereditary fiefs, had become a double danger to the monarchy, he used his power, the alliance of some of the greater vassals and the weakness of the others, to accomplish the process begun by his grandfather of dislodging from their administrative authority the holders of the five traditional posts. Three he reduced to insignificance by conferring the posts on barons of lesser degree : two he practically abolished. He made himself a sovereign uncontrolled by a traditional hierarchy of officialism, and called to his side such personal friends as his own inclination or sagacity might select. He used their advice, but he conferred on them no office which by its constitutional position should give them any right of practical control. Thus Philip of Flanders, Henry II., his uncle, William of Rheims, were, in turn, the advisers of his youth ; and in his manhood he called to his side his faithful friend, brother Guèrin, wise bishop and gallant knight.

But if Philip chose to permanently employ no great official who might become his rival, he surrounded himself with a crowd of *amici, familiares*, counsellors, who did his business, ran his errands, advised him, judged for him, and were his soldiers and diplomatists. These were men, as a rule, chosen from the clergy and the lesser nobility, *novi homines*, who owed all to their master and could be trusted to stand loyally by his side. Chaplains some of them were, some men em-

ployed in household offices, men whom the king had
come to know, whose capacity he had tested and whose
errors he could easily punish.   By such agents the
chief work of the reign was done.   But Philip did not
altogether neglect the traditional methods of government.   The ancient court of barons (*curia, colloquia,
concilium*), called together by personal writs of summons,
met on great occasions to advise the king in the exercise
of all his sovereign acts.   Such a writ was imperative.
Barons, however mighty, who refused to attend, placed
themselves outside the law and declared themselves
the king's enemies.   Thus the Council of Soissons
in the hour of Philip's greatest danger showed on
whom he could rely, and which of his men were gone
over to his foes.   The great councils were military
gatherings as well as mere "parliaments."   The vassals
came with armed knights, and the assemblies were
often largely of the nature of definite preparations for
immediate war.   Questions of war and peace were
debated there, no less than marriage alliances and
matters of feudal law and custom.

But the assemblies, however important their delibera-
tions, had clearly no constitutional rights which they
could enforce against the sovereign.   Their sessions were
not regular, fixed, periodical.   The barons came only in
virtue of the king's summons, and they were summoned
when the king's necessities required.   Need—the need
of moral or material support—not constitutional law,
determined the sessions of the great council.   The real
power belonged to the king and the inner body of his
friends and servants, who carried out the acts to which
the larger assembly gave assent.   Sometimes opposition

in the great council, as in 1188 (and perhaps 1209, when sub-infeudation was forbidden, as in England by Edward I.'s *Quia Emptores*), was successful, and the king withdrew his proposition or exempted certain districts from its operations; but the council rather deliberated than decreed. Still Philip could hardly have dispensed with the great gathering of his barons. By them he was able to gauge the opinion of the feudal and ecclesiastical estates, without whose support it was in the long run impossible for him to act. Strong king he was, but he was strong in spite not in consequence of the assistance of his vassals.

As great council, the most important work of the magnates lay in judicial business. They sat also in the *curia regis*, a smaller body, to which men learned in the law, with no definite feudal qualification, were added. As sovereign the king was supreme judge over his subjects, as suzerain over his vassals, but in each case he was advised by persons feudally or personally related to himself. The court was thus attended by barons, but it was the king's court, not theirs. It sat where he was. It met when he ordered. Of its procedure an excellent example may be found in a writ assigning the castle of Vertaizon to the bishop of Clermont.

"Be it known, etc. That on account of the plaint which our beloved and faithful Robert, bishop of Clermont, lays before us concerning Pontius de Chapteuil and Jarentona his wife, with our own lips we summoned them to Senlis, and appointed a day on which he and his wife should appear in our presence to give an adequate answer to the plaint of the bishop. On this day they neither came nor sent representatives. A

second time, when we were at Châteauroux, we
had them summoned, and appointed a day on account
of the aforesaid plaint, on which day the aforesaid
Pontius came not; his wife came, but came not as she
ought. A third time we summoned the wife by word
of mouth, and had Pontius her husband summoned by
a trusty messenger, and fixed a certain day on which
they were to come to make answer before Hugh de la
Chapelle, our bailiff. On this day they neither came nor
sent representatives, but informed us by letter that
they would make answer on that plaint before the king
of Aragon. The bishop, however, appeared in his own
person on each of the aforementioned days, prepared to
show that Pontius the bishop's liege man and Jarentona
his wife had in the castle of Vertaizon, which they held
on oath from him, treacherously and deceitfully received
by night the bishop's notorious enemies with a view to
seizing his person and destroying his followers. For
this reason, after taking counsel with our barons, we
have assigned the castle with all that appertains thereto
to the bishop and church of Clermont, to hold from us
and our heirs in perpetual tenure in the same way as
our other crown lands, demesne as demesne, fief as fief.
Of the castle and its adjoining land we have publicly
seized the bishop, of demesne as demesne, of fief as fief."

The writ is dated at Paris in January 1205. It
shows the personal character still retained in theory by
the royal jurisdiction. A personal complaint to the
king is personally investigated. And the claim of the
court is wide. The king's power is more than that of a
mere feudal overlord. There is a distinct reminiscence
of the imperial claims of the Karlings.

The court claimed jurisdiction over certain ecclesiastical suits, over cases which concerned the towns and the new communes, and over causes in which the lay feudatories were especially engaged. The larger part of the suits judged by the curia were complaints of robbery against barons by ecclesiastics, and individual barons, whenever they were strong enough, refused to recognise its authority and fought against it. They put forward too the courts of their immediate superior as challenging the exclusive claim of the court of the suzerain, and introduced as a last resort tribunals of arbitration, to which during the last half of the twelfth century many disputes concerning succession and territorial rights were submitted.

The composition of the curia, when it was engaged in judicial business, shows that it was merely the great council in another aspect. In principle there were no judges properly so called. The king was supreme judge ; his vassals assisted him with their advice. The common formula of decision states that cases had been adjudged "in the presence of the king and the magnates of the kingdom." Barons, bishops, abbats, sat as they sat in the great council, to assist in judgment as they sat to assist in deliberation. Sometimes Philip would call for the especial assistance of certain bishops, if the suit were ecclesiastical. More often he would be advised by the officials of the household or the clerks whom Innocent III. himself recognised as learned in both civil and canon law. During the last years of Louis VII. the presence of the king's personal attendants, *familiares, palatini*, had become much more constant; and the names of the chancellor and treasurer, and certain

counsellors or clerks, constantly recur in the signatures
to the judgments. Further, the king would commit to
them authority to judge in his name and in his absence.
Thus there grew up a class of recognised legal officials,
and from that time the phrase *judices nostri* constantly occurs in royal acts. The members of the court
who were qualified by personal knowledge and legal
training became sharply distinguished from those whose
qualification was merely feudal. The curia was gradually turning from a feudal body into something
resembling a modern law-court. Its procedure at the
same time, and by the same process, underwent an
important alteration. The judicial combat was gradually
discouraged. In town charters it was frequently, at
least in trivial matters, definitely forbidden; and the
introduction of written evidence, with the presence of
educated men skilled in the sifting of testimony, tended
to still further minimise the importance of the feudal
element in law and among its administrators. Philip
himself did his utmost to discourage both the ordeal
and the wager of battle, and to gradually substitute the
more civilised methods of inquest and declaration on
oath. While the real importance of the *curia regis* as a
judicial body was thus coming to consist in its practical
elimination of the feudal element from among its members,
it might seem that in a different manner Philip was
giving to the judicial powers of the great vassals an importance which they had not previously possessed. The
reign of Philip Augustus is the first period at which we
can distinctly say that the court of peers assumes a
definite position in French constitutional history.

In one sense, it is true, the *curia regis* must always

have been a court of peers. The barons who attended were the peers of each other, and by custom at least each of them claimed that he could only be judged by his equals. Cases of this claim are frequent enough in the earlier reigns. Suits between barons were tried in the king's courts before the barons who were their peers. In 1153 Louis VII. judged between the duke of Burgundy and the bishop of Langres, to whom he had refused to perform his feudal obligations. He judged in the presence of the archbishops, bishops, and barons who formed the royal court. Yet none of those present, as it happens, save the parties to the suit, were peers of France in the sense in which the term was used later. The recognised right of a baron to be judged by his peers meant in practice a trial in the *curia regis*. But before long a restricted meaning came to be attached to the term peer when it was qualified by the addition of France. As early as 1171 Peter Bernard, prior of Grandmont, is found writing to Henry II. and speaking of Henry, duke and archbishop of Rheims, *peer of France*. Practical politics and legendary sentiment had created before the death of Philip Augustus the famous court of the twelve peers of France. At what date this occurred it is impossible precisely to say. Louis VIII. in his invasion of England in 1216 declared that John was condemned in 1202 by his peers for the murder of Arthur. The statement itself was untrue, and the court by which John was condemned on the charges made against him by his Poitevin vassals was the ordinary court of the suzerain, the *curia regis* at which the barons attended, peers of John in his capacity as Philip's vassal. The "twelve peers of France" certainly could not have appeared on the occasion. The six ecclesiastical peers could not join in a question of blood. Of the lay peers John himself was both duke of Normandy and duke of Aquitaine, the count of Toulouse was his friend, the count of Flanders was abroad, the count of Champagne an infant: only the duke of Burgundy remained. But if, as would appear, John was not condemned to death, the ecclesiastical peers could have attended, and some of the ecclesiastical peers of France were as a matter of fact present. His condemnation, however, as is clear from the objection taken to it by Innocent III., was pronounced by the French king's barons —not by a small and special court. In July 1216 Philip is found judging the claim of Blanche of Navarre and her son Thibault to the county of Navarre, and in the judgment appear the names of "peers of our realm, the prelates of Rheims, Langres, Châlons, Beauvais, Noyon, and the duke of Burgundy"—all those of the "twelve peers" who could have been present. From that date the court of peers of France may be regarded as having been established. There are later instances within a few years, and at the end of the thirteenth century there is demonstrative proof of its constitution. The twelve peers were the dukes of Normandy, Aquitaine, Burgundy, the counts of Flanders, Champagne, Toulouse, the archbishop of Rheims, and the bishops of Langres, Laon, Beauvais, Noyon, Châlons, who were counts or dukes as well as prelates. The political importance of these great personages naturally placed them above the ordinary attendants of the *curia regis*, while their distance from the centre of the French king's power, and their position as the direct vassals, for large tracts of territory, of the crown, marked them out as standing in an exceptional relation to the monarchy. Practical differences were accentuated and stereotyped by the influence of literary sentiment. It was the delight of the literary men who formed part of the court of Philip the Conqueror to compare him with Charles the Great. No analogies were too fanciful, no legends too precarious, to be used in the process which surrounded the thirteenth-century Augustus with the romantic environment of the reviver of the Empire. The song of Roland and the pilgrimage of Charlemagne were read side by side with the verses in which court poets were striving to immortalise their sovereign and themselves. No legend of Charlemagne was more famous than that which surrounded him with twelve peers, the great vassals of the Empire and the heroic companions of his doughty deeds. Should not the new Augustus too have his twelve peers of France? They were naturally marked out among the great feudatories, six great churchmen and six great barons. They were each other's peers, and the medieval theory, so persistent in its influence on every side of life, that a man could only be judged by his equals, gave to them a sort of natural and exclusive right to be each other's judges under the presidency of the sovereign. Thus by Philip's death the French kings were surrounded by their twelve peers, who stood with romantic but mostly intangible privileges separating them from the lesser vassals outside the royal domain. The dignity of the monarchy was enhanced, and its practical power was indirectly increased by the creation of the court, and still more by the sentiment so largely responsible for its creation.

Thus stood the monarchy of Philip Augustus in relation to church and barons. An advance even more significant is to be seen in the king's connection with the commercial classes.

The relations between the Capetian kings and the trading and popular classes may best be observed in general by a study of their attitude towards the growth of the new urban constitution, the commune, and in particular by observation of their intimate association with their own chief city Paris. The ancient liberties of the south, surviving at least in sentiment from Roman times the privileges granted by the house of Anjou to the towns in their territories, represent two different types of municipal organisation with which Philip during the earlier part of his reign was not concerned. The part of Gaul over which he had influence was the north and the centre : and here we must examine the work of his predecessors as a preparation for his own. A clear distinction is to be observed between the attitude of the Capetian kings towards the growth of municipal liberties within, and outside, their own domain. In the first case the kings were concerned primarily as direct lords, in the second primarily as suzerains. As lords, the kings behaved as did other feudal superiors. An extension of liberties seemed necessarily to imply an encroachment on their own powers. They were therefore almost always opposed to the growth of communes.

The twelfth century saw a large development in action of the principle of association. Commerce, police, politics, all took advantage of it. Trade guilds, associations of merchants, created the great routes and

founded international commerce. The obligations of
law were brought home to the people by systems of
close local assurance. The Peace of God, proclaimed by
the great society of the Church, was enforced by courts
whose sanction was almost solely that of mutual assent
and forbearance. Even in 1182 there was founded in
Velai the confraternity of the *Encapuchonnés*, joined by
"many bishops and magnates, nobles, and men of lower
degree." The associations for the preservation of the
peace did not die out indeed before the end of the
thirteenth century, and in the more directly political
sphere they have a parallel in the associations formed
between barons for the enforcement of their rights in
relation to their suzerain, and the system of mutual
sureties which the kings were eager to institute among
their vassals. In France, as in Spain, the spirit which
founded and animated the *Juntas* was prominent. In
local organisation the spirit manifested itself in the
growth of united bodies within the towns of the north
and centre which opposed an united front to their lords,
lay or clerk, and obtained from them the concession of
a charter which recognised the town as a commune, a
self-governing unit, entering as one body into the feudal
hierarchy and dealing as one with all outside powers.
The grant of the communal privileges was the recognition of the complete unity of the town in internal
government. It freed the citizens from the arbitrary
treatment of the lords, and placed them in possession of
definite privileges and rights which law could recognise
and perhaps enforce.

From the point of view of the kings, the growth of
communes outside their own lands was of direct

advantage to the royal authority. It limited the
power of the feudal hierarchy, and it created a new
class with whom direct relations could be held. Thus
in the case of a vacancy in a bishopric or great abbey
the kings used their privileges—of *regale* or otherwise—to encourage the growth of urban liberties ;
and they interfered constantly in behalf of privileges
which the prelates contested and endeavoured to limit.
Towards lay fiefs, and especially those of the great
feudatories, a strong and consistent policy was difficult.
The power of the suzerain could but rarely be used, but
there were occasions when the king might justly claim
to interfere against an oppressive lord, and these
occasions were not neglected. The growth of legal
science too, and the delight in definitions which spread
from the philosophy of the day into practical life,
encouraged the kings to assert the right of confirming
the creation of all new communes, and even to declare
that all towns in which a commune was instituted
became *ipso facto* royal towns.

But while kings watched the growth of urban
privileges with mingled feelings, the father of Philip
Augustus had begun the policy of creating new towns as
a counterpoise to the power of the local lords. During
the last thirty years of his reign he multiplied *villes
neuves*, endowing them with liberal privileges to be
enjoyed under his sole protection, stipulating for the
payment of dues, and making free men of all villeins
who should take refuge within their bounds. Ville-
neuve-le-roi in the Sénonais received, in 1163, the
charter of Lorris. Many others followed. The policy
was one which Philip developed. As the twelfth century

drew on, the kings became more able to assert their
independence of the feudal classes, and more com-
petent to carry out the policy which they had already
planned.   At this stage of affairs Philip succeeded
his father, and the monarchy passed, in regard to the
communes, from a period of hesitating support to one
of definite alliance.   An illustration may be found in
the famous history of the commune of the Laonnais.
Side by side with the urban communes rural organisa-
tions were springing up which claimed, and won, the
same privileges.   Of these the commune of the Laonnais
is a typical example.   In the domains of the bishop
which surrounded the ancient city of the Karling kings
were seventeen villages which attached themselves to
the little town of Anizi-le-Château as a centre.   The
villagers were serfs of the bishops, and villeins of more or
less free condition.   During the vacancy of the bishopric,
1174-1175, the peasants, now for the time under the
direct rule of the crown, applied to Louis VII. for a
charter similar to that which the burgesses of the city
of Laon enjoyed, and which had already been won by
other rural associations.   The king, paid, there is no
doubt, for his compliance, granted a charter which
incorporated the villages, and gave them, in consideration
of a small yearly rent from each household, definite
rights against the bishop, their lord.   No sooner was a
new bishop in possession of the see than he repudiated
with indignation the encroachment on his rights and the
rights of the Church of Laon.   He demanded the withdrawal of a charter which the king had no right to grant.
He appealed to the Pope.   He took up arms to destroy
the commune.   Before the summer of 1177 was over the

commune of the Laonnais had ceased to exist. Weak as
he was, Louis VII. could not tamely submit to such an
insult. He marched into the district, compelled the
bishop to submit and to fly. But this was by no means
the end. The count of Hainault, kinsman of the dispossessed bishop of Laon, intervened, and the quarrel
merged in the great political struggle in which Louis
VII. was engaged. The king accepted the bishop's
submission, but the bishop was already accused of
murder in the course of his suppression of the commune,
and it was a year before he was freed from the charge.
Then suddenly, by the marriage of Philip Augustus
with the count of Hainault's daughter, the bishop was
admitted again into the king's favour. The commune
was dissolved, the villeins were sacrificed, Louis VII.
himself was humiliated, by a political necessity. In
1180 the bishop of Laon married young Philip to his
kinswoman Elizabeth, and for five years no more is
heard of the villeins of the Laonnais. In 1185 the
exactions of the restored bishop had become insup-
portable. Philip himself was compelled—or was, it
may be, eager — to intervene. He fixed the tallage
which the men of the Laonnais should pay to the
bishop, and their dues to the vidame and the bishop,
and he placed over them twelve officers chosen from
among themselves, who should judge of all differences
that might arise between them and the bishop. This
was a step towards the re-establishment of the commune.
Five years later we find the commune in existence.
Philip at Paris, in June 1190, promises to settle the
matter of the commune of the Laonnais if requested by
the bishop or the Church of Laon within a year of his

return from the East. If he dies during his absence the commune is to be destroyed. A few months later, at Messina, he definitely abolished it—a curious commentary on the strength of the influence of the Church on those engaged in crusade. Philip, whose sympathies, as well as his interests, had clearly gone with rural liberties outside his domain, was compelled to give way to a force too strong to resist. The young Capetian king bowed to the power which had raised his ancestor to the throne. The later history of the Laonnais runs on different lines. For ten years more the peasants bore the oppression of the bishop. In 1204 a number of fugitives were gladly received within the territory of Enguerran III. of Couci; but the bishop protested against this invasion of his feudal rights, and the unhappy villeins had to return. Two years later a quarrel between the bishop and his chapter gave new hope to the peasants. The canons already at feud with their prelate accused him of ill-treating his serfs. The metropolitan chapter of Rheims judged as arbiter between them, and compelled the bishop to restore to the peasants their fixity of tallage (recognised in 1185), and to submit all disputes to the judgment of his chapter. Here, as far as the reign of Philip is concerned, our information ends. The case is typical of the difficulties with which the kings had to contend in their dealings with the movement towards refranchisement. Themselves willing to do anything to increase privileges which should ally new associations to themselves, they were often overcome by the strength of the feudal organisation which they would have gladly depressed.

An examination of Philip's legal acts shows how

constantly he was concerned in this contest between feudalism and extra-feudal association. Twenty cases of intervention between the years 1182 and 1220 may thus be summarised. In 1182 Philip confirmed the charter which he had granted to the townsmen of Corbie, and which the abbat had endeavoured to revoke. In 1190 he intervened in a dispute between commune and abbat, and promised a final settlement on his return from the crusade. At Messina, a few months later, as in the case of the Laonnais, he gave a new decision—this time that the commune should remain as it was in his father's day, annulling all innovations prejudicial to the abbey. In 1183 he confirmed a decision of his grandfather to repress the unjust pretentions of the commune of Soissons. In 1184 he suppressed the commune of Châteauneuf de Tours, just then fallen into his hands. In 1187, probably, he first guaranteed large liberties to his citizens of Orleans "to take away the burden of the city." These gave considerable powers to the burghers both against his own prévôt and against their serfs. In February 1192 he granted a commune to Hesdin, in Artois, and accepted a composition for his annual dues from the commune of Noyon. He intervened later, in 1196 and 1223, between the bishop and the commune of this city; and he also issued an ordinance, undated, which is of extreme importance in the history of the judicial power of the *curia regis*. He ordered that if the bishop should have a complaint against the commune or any member of it, it should be adjudicated by freemen of the bishop, and if the judgment should be accepted by the commune it should stand firm; if not, appeal should lie to the king, and the *curia* should issue a final judgment. In 1193 he intervened to define the rights of the abbat of S. Pierre-le-Vif and the commune of Sens. In 1194 he declared the rights and customs of the citizens of Arras, and in the next year he warned the mayor, échevins, and jurés of that city to make no encroachment on the rights of the Church. In the same year he is found recognising the existence of the commune of Étampes, which he suppressed in 1199. In 1200 he made an order regarding the collection of tallages in Bapaume by the mayor, échevins, and jurés. In 1201 he confirmed all the hansas (guilds) of Mantes, and granted the prévôtship to the mayor and commune at a rent of 1100 livres parisis. In 1202 he banished from his realm certain offenders against the commune of Laon, and forgave to the commune any grievances he might have against it. Thirteen years later he confirmed an agreement between the same commune and the chapter. In 1204 he granted a commune to the inhabitants of Andely, which he had just taken, but the privileges given to win their loyalty were not continued when there was no further danger of an attack on Normandy. In 1204 he gave to the commune of Poitiers the statutes of the Rouen commune, a type the least free of any that were granted, and one which the French kings readily followed when they had acquired the Norman capital. Fillièvre received a commune in 1205, and in the same year the commune of Chaumont, near Beauvais, won the lease of the prévôtship. Cappi, near Péronne, about the same time received a commune on the northern model, and a similar one was granted to Athies in 1211. In 1209 the king confirmed the agreement between the count and the commune of

Montreuil. In 1209 he confirmed his father's charter to Compiègne, and he frequently intervened to recognise settlements between the abbat and the commune. In 1214, 1217, 1218, he recognised the privileges of Péronne. In 1220 he leased his windmills at Crépi to the commune.

Many other instances might be given. It might be shown how ready was Philip to confirm existing charters, and license them in the royal registers, as when he confirmed the charter of Amiens in 1185 ; how gladly he gave the right of association, taking care to base it on principles the most favourable to his own position as lord, as when in 1204 he sent to the inhabitants of Niort, in Poitou (whom King John had already recognised as having a commune), the établissements of Rouen as a model for their communal organisation ; how he made it a practice from the beginning of his reign to grant privileges to all towns which he added to his dominions, as to Tournai in 1187 ; how carefully he considered local circumstances before he issued each particular grant, as in the case of the modifications of the charter of Mantes when its privileges were bestowed on Chaumont and on Pontoise. But enough has been said to enable us to reach some conclusions with regard to the nature of the urban and rural constitutions which were obtained during the reign of Philip Augustus and to the character of the privileges which they involved, and to estimate the personal relation of the king to the movement towards enfranchisement.

From the charters granted or confirmed by Philip Augustus at least three types emerge. Of the south, since Philip had practically no relations with its towns, we need not speak. First, in the north, where all trace of Roman municipal organisation had perished, and where the inhabitants of the towns were exposed to the opposition of a strong baronage and a powerful array of great prelates, the victory of the citizens was won through the progress of commerce and the development of industrial forces. Along the great trade route from Italy through Germany and Flanders there grew up in the cities associations of merchants and craftsmen, who became rich through commerce, and ·united through common interest, and who sealed their commercial success by winning political power. From city to city spread the ideas which guilds and trades' unions fostered, and the northern French cities took example from their neighbours under the emperor or the count of Flanders. The townsmen banded together to "swear the commune." The charters won from baron or bishop naturally show traces of the importance of commercial considerations, but they bear witness also to the wide scope of the movement and the strength of the cities of the north. The great town halls that in northern France, as in Flanders, still testify to the dignity of the mercantile corporations, fitly represent the pride and power of the bourgeois in the new constitutions. Every inhabitant in the town was obliged to swear to the commune. Only those were fully citizens who had a house within the town. As a unit the commune stood side by side with baron and bishop in the feudal hierarchy. It had right of justice, right of making war, with its own army, its own fortifications, and city-chest. The commune generally, if not always, implies a mayor. He was assisted by a number of échevins or of jurés, the

successors of the Karling *scabini*, or the presumed
representatives of those who had first sworn to the
constitution.

The greater part of this northern region lay outside
the direct domain of the French king, and his attitude
towards particular efforts for emancipation was affected
by circumstances, as in the case of the commune of the
Laonnais. In the centre of Gaul, and within the
domains of the French king, a different type of constitution was obtained. The citizens were not strong
enough to win their rights at the point of the sword,
or to enforce them by the power of their commercial
supremacy. The type of the urban charters of this
district has been found in the charter granted by Louis
VII. to the little town of Lorris. Here the villeins
become the king's burghers. Their dues to the crown
are defined, their liability to taxation, purveyance,
custom-dues, and the like, strictly limited. While they
have no such complete self-government as the communes
of the north, they are under none of the dangers which
the right to make peace and war, the power to make
alliances with great potentates, involve. The charter
of Lorris proved popular among both barons and villeins.
It was largely copied. Paris itself was the supreme
example of its use.

In the west, in Normandy, Poitou, Saintonge, and the
more northern lands of the house of Henry II. the type
is that of the établissements given by that great king
in Rouen. Here the liberties granted were more
restricted than in north or centre. A hundred peers
chose every year twenty-four jurés, twelve of whom
were échevins and twelve counsellors, to administer

justice. From three candidates presented by the peers the king chose a mayor : and within the town the king maintained his own officers. To the king alone did the "haute justice" belong, and by him alone could the militia be called out.

Such were the general types of urban constitution with which Philip had to deal. His attitude towards them determined in no small degree the future of the French monarchy. Where his father and grandfather had never been more than half favourable he became definitely friendly, and thus he prepared for his grandson the period of subjugation, by which the towns became the absolute property of the sovereign. The most significant expression of the general aims which directed Philip's policy towards the communes is to be obtained, perhaps, from two special methods which he adopted. Following the example of his father he frequently associated himself with a local lord in the possession of his domain by contracts of *pariage*, wherein rights were shared. This gave many opportunities of interference to the crown and tended to place the barons more and more under the king's control. In a similar way *letters of protection* were issued, which placed a particular town under the direct political authority of the crown. Then without in either case granting charters the king came to share rights and to exercise authority—a position of which he knew well how to avail himself, and which his successors extended into still more definite domination. In Philip's action a definite policy may be traced. He continued communal organisation in Corbie, Soissons, Noyon, Compiègne, Laon, S. Riquier, Senlis, Beauvais, and many other

towns, taking part with the citizens against local lords
and prelates. Thus he raised up against the nobles a
new estate pledged to alliance with the crown. Within
the lands which he added to his domain, or of which
he obtained influence, he confirmed the charters which
had been already granted,—in Vermandois, Artois, and
Flanders the widest municipal liberties, and in the lands
won from the Angevin house the lesser privileges which
the Norman dukes and counts of Anjou had conferred.
He did more. Not only did he confirm old grants:
he constantly founded new communes, and that, contrary to the custom of his father, within his own
domain.

For this new policy three reasons have been assigned.
First, the military importance of the communes must be
observed. Their troops, it is true, were by no means of
first-rate capacity. At Bouvines, though the militia of
many northern communes, not least the men of Arras,
Beauvais, Amiens, and Compiègne, stood in front of the
king, exposed to the charge of the German knights,
they stood there simply to be beaten. But if they were
no more than "food for powder"—if the anachronism
be allowed—in the field, they at least served to guard
fortresses, to man their own walls, and oppose a stout
resistance to the march of an invading army. A
second reason, probably still more powerful, may be
found in the king's pecuniary needs. Every concession
meant a gain in hard cash. Philip's treasury underwent an extraordinary strain. The long struggle
with the Plantagenets, the policy of diplomacy and
aggression, the negotiations and quarrels with Rome,
all meant a large demand; and chief among the sources

to which he could turn to replenish his coffers were the
towns.   If they won their liberties, they paid for them.
The third reason has already been touched upon in
passing.   In the new communes the crown found a new
political ally against great prelates and great barons.
With the growth of feudal privilege, and the tendency
towards the feudalisation of every office, the relations
between the great estates and the crown had undergone
a perilous change.   Philip called a new estate into
existence to redress the balance of the old.

But it would be greatly to underrate the conqueror's ability to restrict his reasons to such as
these.   His foresight and his grasp of principle were
rare among medieval sovereigns.   He saw, there can
be no doubt, with a true statesman's eye, into the
future.   He had some conception of what liberty meant,
and what equality.   He was more than a feudal
monarch.   While he was founding absolutism he was
destroying hundreds of petty tyrannies.   Though he
was a feudal sovereign, he has some claims to be
considered a king of the people.   With his astuteness
and craft were mingled many popular gifts.   If he was
"well-beloved," he certainly, after his own fashion,
loved his people, and among the glories of his reign his
relations with the urban communities was perhaps the
greatest and the most lasting.

If Philip was a king with a purpose in regard to all
the towns, most especially had he a purpose in regard
to Paris.   Paris, the home of the Capetian kings, had
not escaped the influence of the great movement of the
age.   There the ancient corporation of *nautæ Parisienses*
had survived from Roman times, and was still, under

the title of *marchands de l'eau, mercatores aquæ*, at the
head of the commercial life of the city.   It was to this
body that the kings granted charters with privileges for
the city.   In 1121 Louis VI., in 1170 Louis VII., gave
special rights and special statutes.   The privileges
recognised were declared to descend from ancient times.
They placed the whole trade of the city under the
direction of the ancient corporation.   The guild system
in its fullest development was represented in Paris
by the triumph of the *marchands de l'eau*.   On the
corporation thus recognised, the kings relied in all their
subsequent difficulties, and Philip followed up the
policy of his predecessors by special favours and
special grants.   He first took in hand the work of
making Paris a great city.   He first paved the streets
and surrounded the city with fortified walls.   "It
happened that after certain days King Philip, *semper
Augustus*, making some stay in Paris, was pondering on
the business of his realm as he walked in his palace,
and coming to a window whence he would often for
pleasure look upon the Seine, he observed how the
carriages passing through the mire stirred up the mud,
whence issued a horrible stench.   Determined not to
endure this, he thought out an arduous but necessary
work, which none of his predecessors, whether from its
great difficulty or its cost, had dared to undertake.
He called together the burghers with the prévôt of the
city, and ordered by royal authority that all the streets
and ways of the whole city of Paris should be paved
with hard and strong stones."   So Rigord tells the tale,
and he adds in the true medieval spirit that the city
which had been called Lutea (Lutetia) from the stench

of its mud, was now named Paris after Priam's son, the ancestor of the Frankish kings.

The city then was ruled by a royal prévôt, the officer who guarded the royal rights in the king's domains. By his side stood the great corporation by which so much of the work that Philip ordered was carried out. In recognition of their labours on the streets and the walls, they received in 1192 enlarged privileges, by which their monopoly of the traffic of the Seine was rendered more stringent. Further privileges were also granted to the *marchands de l'eau*. In 1213 they received the right to exact dues from every boat which touched at the great bridge of Paris. The weights and measures were also placed under their direction, with the right of jurisdiction over all cases which arose in connection with it. For the constitution of the city itself Philip had made an important provision in the directions before his departure for the crusade. While in other places he set up a council of four "prudent, lawful, and well-esteemed men" to advise the prévôt, in Paris he put six, and these members, it would appear, of his own council. Thus Paris never received the full privileges of self-government. It was never a commune : it remained under the royal prévôt. But the council of six burghers, without whose advice the prévôt could not act, both conferred considerable powers upon the citizens, and prepared the way for the final establishment of a permanent municipality under S. Louis.

How far the prévôtship had become under Philip a saleable office it is impossible to say. It is probable that the king took large gifts from the men he appointed, and that he chose as his representatives persons well acquainted with the trade of the city; but it is unlikely that the post was actually put up for sale among the citizens as Joinville declares it was before the reforms of S. Louis.

Philip may claim then to be the founder of the medieval Paris. Not only did he begin the paving of the principal streets, but he founded the great markets, and gave the city protection through the fortified wall and the erection of the " grand " and " petit " châtelets. Like many of the monarchs of his time he was a great builder. Many a city owes its wall, its castles, its chief churches to his inspiration—many a little village has a church endowed or built by his hand. He took in hand the beautifying of towns : under him town life was to become pleasant, luxurious, as well as secure. And in Paris, while the military knights erected the Temple, and the bishop began the matchless church of Notre Dame, Philip set up outside the city the Louvre which should have so famous a history. An enthusiastic biographer, not altogether without foundation, might call Paris the creation of Philip the Conqueror. If Philip was thus careful of his chief city, he was no less the patron of the great University that was springing up in its midst. It was Philip who gave to the masters and scholars their first charter of privilege. After the tumult of 1200, when several of the students were slain by citizens, Philip took stern vengeance. He ordered that any person found ill-treating a student should be arrested by the first passer-by and delivered to instant justice, and from such offenders he took away the right of recourse to the ordeal or to wager of battle.

All scholars he admitted to privilege of clergy, thus placing them under the judgment of ecclesiastical tribunals alone. In the universities, as he saw, were rising up strong and firm supports of the monarchic claims. The contests of the schoolmen, the passionate pursuit of reality through the shifting mirage of intangible phenomena, were training thinkers who should find moral bases for the assertions of royal power. Theologians were debating theories which gave traditional and scriptural support to the assumptions of the crown, and lawyers were elaborating a science which should confirm the sovereign as the source and centre of all authority.

This survey of the different estates and classes with which the crown was brought into relation, and of Philip's policy towards them, aids us in estimating the difficulties, as well as the strength, of the monarchy in the early thirteenth century. But no picture of the social order would be complete which did not take account of the general spirit of lawlessness which accompanied the gradual decay of the feudal system. France, even more than other nations, was year by year in different districts the prey of wandering bands of disbanded soldiers, mercenaries discharged after a short campaign, and petty knights who had little to lose by almost avowedly assuming the life of freebooters. The constant wars between small feudal lords, merging into or shooting off from the great racial or dynastic hostilities, covered the country with reckless warriors, whose whole work was fighting, and whose hand was against every man. Soon every man's hand was against them. From Rome and in many a local synod the Church put forth anathemas. The kings crushed, whenever they had the chance, with heavy hand. Voluntary associations sprang up to enforce the Peace and the Truce of God, the pathetic fictions by which the eleventh century had endeavoured, if not to heal its wounds, at least to prevent their spreading into a general disease. After the Lateran council of 1179 had formally excommunicated the Brabançons, Bragmanni, Cotteraux, or by whatever malicious or barbarous name they should be called, a new zest was given to the war of God in which the blood-stained brigands were put down without mercy by the sword. At Notre Dame de Puy en Velai, a famous centre of pilgrimage, a carpenter named Durand had a vision which bade him raise a new society to check the outrages and bring back the peace of God. Bishops and clerks, barons and their vassals, listened to him with amazement and conviction. The Society of the Brothers of God's Peace, or White Hoods, sprang up, which first set itself to make peace in Southern Gaul, and then to suppress at the sword's point the bands of murderers from whom every district had suffered. As patron of such societies, as general champion of the poor clerks and the oppressed peasants, the king had a great opportunity, and Philip took advantage of it to the full.

A survey of the position of the monarchy during the years 1180 to 1223 shows that it advanced not merely by conquest and political intrigue, but by the natural growth of institutions, by the influence of a philosophy which sought for a representative of abstract unity, and by the progress of commerce which looked to the crown for support and privilege. Philip called himself the Protector of the Church and of the People, as well as

Conqueror and Augustus. The strength of his power lay in the growing sense of the protection which it afforded, and in the wisdom with which he carried into action the principles which were to command the future.

CHAPTER VI

PHILIP AND THE PAPACY

BESET on all sides by dangers within and without, it would have been well if Philip could have relied upon strong moral forces to support him. A virtuous king of the Franks, aggressive and masterful in his own ambitions, yet a Crusader and a traditional guardian of the churches, might have relied on the assistance which the spiritual power at the centre of European politics could give in many and important ways. But Philip's character did not run after the fashion which popes would approve. A man of hot passion and invincible obstinacy, he was determined to have and to hold whatever his fancy desired. And it was his fortune to meet as an antagonist on a question of simplest Christian morals one of the greatest men who ever sat in the chair of S. Peter.

Philip's first wife, Elizabeth, died on March 15, 1190, leaving him the son who was to be Louis VIII. The crusade gave short time for his regrets. Three months after she had been laid to rest in Notre Dame, Philip was taking his standard from S. Denys. On his return he was deep in plots and treaties against Richard

of England. His first wife had given him a politic
alliance. Why should he not seek a new support with a
second spouse? France and Denmark had already close
intercourse. Shakespeare, when he sent Laertes to Paris,
was rightly representing the custom of the twelfth
century. Many a Dansker had studied in learning or
in war or the arts of polite life at the capital of the
Frankish king: a Danish college received the young
sojourners from the north. Denmark itself was winning
back some of the fame in Europe which the great Cnut
had given it. Alliances with Germany were constant,
and with England the Danish king had now a family
connexion. Cnut VI. married the daughter of Henry the
Lion of Saxony. He was thus by marriage the nephew
of Richard I. His father Waldemar had left several
daughters. Of these the second, Ingeborgis, was "beautiful
in face, more beautiful in soul," and not, it would seem,
more than eighteen years old. For her hand Philip in
the spring of 1193 sent an embassage to ask,—Stephen,
bishop of Noyon at its head, the son of that Walter the
sub-chamberlain, who stood for so many years at the
king's right hand. Cnut received the ambassadors with
barbaric splendour and their request with undissembled
delight. "What," said he, "will your master ask as
dower?" "The right of Denmark to England, and for a
year the fleet and army of the Danes." The medieval
passion for concrete rights stood out in the request, as it
did in the fantastic claim which Louis VIII. made later
to the English throne. Such rights were as readily
granted as they were easily asked, but to give troops,
with the Wends at his gates, was more than Cnut could
do. Philip might land in England from a Danish fleet,

but the Danish king could not part with his protection,
and was not ready to be embroiled with King Richard.
Ten thousand marks, demanded instead, were given.
The poor king of the North would strain his resources,
he said, to show his sense of the honour of alliance with
the great Philip.   No fear need he now have, replied the
French envoy, of the hatred of the Emperor's men, the
Germans, who proudly took for their own the name of
Rome.   Thus viewed, the marriage is seen to be part of
Philip's general European policy, as well as an illustration
of his hostility to the Angevins.

In the summer Ingeborgis sailed from Denmark
under charge of Peter, bishop of Röskilde, who had
himself studied in France, and with a gallant train.
Philip met her at Amiens, with a great escort of
bishops and barons.   He bestowed on her, as dower,
the dependencies of the prévôtships of Orleans, Chéci,
Châteauneuf, and Neuville.   On the Vigil of the
Assumption, August 14, they were wedded in the great
cathedral.   On the next day the young bride was
crowned by the king's uncle, William of Rheims the
"white-handed," with the bishops, Peter of Arras, John
of Cambray, Thibault of Amiens, Lambert of Térouanne,
and Stephen of Tournai.   Young, timid, utterly ignorant
of the language of her new country, Ingeborgis found
herself, the first day of her married life, the possessor of
the great powers which custom had allowed to the wives
of the Frankish kings : but the happiness of her wedding,
the glory of her coronation, were short-lived.   On the
very day she was crowned queen, her husband cast her
off.   Even while the crowning was being solemnised, he
was seen to tremble and turn pale, and hardly could he

endure till the ceremony was at an end. Chroniclers sought in vain for a reason. Unsavoury details appeared in the letters which the controversy soon produced. Ingeborgis said he was her husband, and she knew not why he hated her. Philip felt some physical loathing, and vowed never to have her for wife.

He may well have thought that to be unwed was as easy as to be wed. It was an age of papal diplomacy, and the mass of Canon Law, so soon as it had time to be investigated by skilled students, was found capable of a thousand interpretations, and yet often so rigid and severe as to demand of necessity a power of dispensation. The Canon Law tied knots so hard that some man sometimes must cut them. The central tribunal of international law, the supreme court of ecclesiastical appeal, was at Rome, and it was not slow to exercise the power which necessity imposed upon it. The Church must have its equity : and it must be administered by a court of trained lawyers. The popes and their curia must interpret and overrule what Gratian and his school had codified. So soon as it was recognised that the rules forbidding marriage within remote degrees of kindred and affinity covered an enormous field of natural and artificial relationship, a power of dispensation became essential, and not less necessary a power which should decree in the last resort how far the rules extended. Philip was impatient of delay. Once again, it is said, he visited the queen as she lay in the house of the abbey of S. Maurdes-Fossés, near Paris. It was indeed an amazing marriage, and concerning its strange incidents, those were wisest who held their tongues.

The king would have sent the unhappy girl home

again, but she would not return. He determined then
to proceed in a formal manner for the dissolution of the
marriage. But he did not at once appeal to the Roman
court. He preferred to win from his own timid prelates
what the popes might deny. On November 4, 1193, a
council of bishops met at Compiègne. Men were ready
to swear that the marriage was void on account of the
near kindred of the parties. Their fathers were of kin,
for Philip I., great-grandfather of the bridegroom was
brother to a Danish princess, ancestress of Ingeborgis.
She was akin, too, to Philip's first wife in at least
two ways, and elaborate pedigrees were prepared—or
concocted. The bishops declared a divorce without
hesitation.

Ingeborgis had in vain appealed for aid to the archbishop of Rheims. She could not speak the tongue of
her persecutors. The sentence reached her only through
interpreters. Her one word was, " Mala Francia, mala
Francia : Roma, Roma." She was sent to the convent
of Beaurepaire, a cell of the house of Cysoing (the scene,
years later, of Philip's greatest victory), and there waited
with prayer and vigil for the judge that should do her
right. Cnut was not slow to plead his injured sister's
cause before Celestine III. She herself appealed, and
the bishop of Tournai endeavoured to arouse some sympathy in the breasts of the French bishops. If Philip
had thought, like so many of his contemporaries, that
everything could be bought at Rome, or if he had relied
upon the ingenuity of the canonists, whom his influence
could reach, he soon found his error. The scandal was
too gross ; and the popes were the champions of injured
women. The Danish envoys easily proved the genea-

logies to be mere fables. Celestine sent a legate to
Philip. The king was obdurate. Then the pope, "as
the common father of all Christians, and the guardian
of the divine rule upon earth, in virtue of the fulness of
the papal power, and with the assent of his brethren,
declared the sentence of divorce to be null and void,
illegal, pronounced against a woman ignorant of the
language of the country and without defence."

Philip showed no sign of submission. He imprisoned
the Danish envoys : he turned a deaf ear to the protests
of pope and bishops : he set about to find a new wife.
Several damsels were suggested. The daughter of Conrad,
count Palatine, refused to marry one who had ill-treated
a noble girl. But another German alliance was found.
Agnes, daughter of the Duke of Meran, niece of the
Margrave of Meissen, in June 1196 became Philip's wife.
Three years passed by in threats and negotiations. New
legates, new gatherings of bishops, new letters from the
aged pope, attempted to deal with this new scandal.
And meantime Ingeborgis remained practically a
prisoner, patiently waiting for justice. She was forced,
it is said, to sell her jewels, her very clothes, to seek
alms. "The king," she wrote to the Holy Father, "can
allege no fault against me, yet he scorns the letters of
your holiness and the mandates of the cardinals. I die
if your pity does not come to my aid." The bishop
of Tournai renewed his appeals on her behalf : even the
white-handed metropolitan of Rheims was touched. But
soon the unhappy queen was to have a stronger defender.

On January 8, 1198, Innocent III., the greatest of
medieval popes, ascended the papal throne. One of his
first acts was to write a formal letter to Philip, announc-

ing his accession, and significantly promising his aid in
all things which belong to God. Immediately afterwards, he wrote with no uncertain sound to the bishop
of Paris: "Whom God hath joined together, let not
man put asunder. We write not this to instruct you,
of whose knowledge in the divine law we are well
informed, but that we should make clear the force of
our intention. By so much as we love our dear son in
Christ, Philip, king of the Franks, and intend to
honour him with our special favour, by so much the
more are we grieved that he should have striven so far
as in him lay to put away our dearest daughter in
Christ, his queen. Wherefore shall you warn him, and
enjoin for the pardon of his sins that he straightway take
to him again the said queen, lest he incur the divine
wrath, and infamy among men, and thereby suffer
irreparable loss." He was not long in writing with
equal directness to Philip himself. He had already
intervened to confirm peace between him and the count
of Flanders. With the charity of a Christian prelate
and the dignity of a sovereign, Innocent spoke of the
glories of France, and the papal affection towards his
dynasty. Then passing swiftly to the scandal of which
all men talked, "I command you," he said, "that you
judge your own acts so that you be not condemned of
others. Recall your lawful wife, and then we will hear
all that you may lawfully urge. If this you do not, no
power shall turn us to right or left till justice be done."
This was the tenor of the letter. It was followed by the
arrival of a legate, Peter of Capua, who was instructed
to insist, under pain of interdict, on the immediate
repudiation of Agnes.

But even popes at the end of the twelfth century could not turn politics as they would, or disentangle moral questions wholly from difficulties of statesmanship. Philip did not yield. Innocent might have immediately excommunicated him. Certainly, but not without involving in a far worse confusion and bloodshed the already dangerous contest between the claimants of the empire, and adding new difficulties in the way of the peace between France and England, which it was the aim of the same legation to produce with a view to the great purpose of Innocent's heart, —a united and successful crusade. Surrounded on every side by war and rumour of war, called to intervene in Germany, Norway, England, Leon, Hungary, Portugal, Innocent was compelled to wait before he took extreme measures against the king of the Franks. Early in 1199 Philip was corresponding with him, pointing out how dangerous would be the election of Otto to the empire, and seeking his support for Philip of Swabia. In sight of the great principles which were involved in the relations between the papacy and the empire, it might seem for the moment as if Innocent forgot the wrongs of Ingeborgis. In any case the legate made no impression upon the French king. For ten months he pursued the affair too tepidly, says a chronicler. And meanwhile Richard of England died, John succeeded, and the cry of the Christians in the East still sounded in the ears of the pope.

At length in October 1199 Innocent wrote a long, clear, and stern appeal to "the archbishops, bishops, abbats, priors, and all the clergy in the realm of France." He declared how illegal had been the divorce, how

great a scandal was Philip's conduct. He adjured the
clergy to use all means to convince the king of his sin.
He announced that the legate should once more warn him,
but if he resisted he should straightway pronounce the
interdict. And this done, the pope ordered all clerks,
under pain of deprivation, to cease from the performance
of every ecclesiastical function. On December 6, 1199,
a council summoned by the legate met at Dijon. The
archbishop of Rheims himself was present, and with
him were the archbishops of Lyons, Besançon, and
Vienne, and many bishops and abbats. Messengers to
the king were refused admission, and he declared that
he had appealed to Rome. But at Rome the question
had already been decided, and the pope's word left no
excuse for delay.

For seven days the council sat. At length, at midnight on the 13th, a solemn procession passed through
the dark and deserted streets to the great cathedral.
For the last time they sang Litany and Miserere ; relics
were hidden away, the reserved Host was consumed,
the altars were stripped, the crucifix covered, the church
wrapped in gloom. Then the legate pronounced an
interdict on all the lands of the Frankish king so long
as his adulterous union with Agnes should continue.
For thirteen days after Christmas should the sentence
remain unpublished, to allow a last hour of repentance.
With groans and tears the dread order was received.
Then there was silence in the cathedral as there should
soon be in every church where the praises of God had
been sung. A few weeks later the sentence was pronounced at Vienne, in the ancient kingdom of Burgundy.
Philip had fallen under the extreme sentence of the

Church. Robert I. and Bertha, Philip I. and Bertrada,
had each incurred the Pope's condemnation. To their
successor came a still greater punishment, for a greater
crime.

On February 5, 1200, the interdict was put in force.
Some clergy, through terror of the king, or love of
their flocks, or striving to be at peace with all men,
would not publish it. Innocent would brook no resistance. On March 11 he wrote again : "The remedy
is harsh in truth, but strong diseases are not cured by
gentle treatment." Some bishops still held out, and
chiefly Hugh of Auxerre, who looked, it was said, for
the archbishopric of Sens. Philip's rage burst out
against those who opposed him. "You bishops, you
care for nought ; so long as you can eat your fat
benefices you care not what becomes of the poor folk.
But have a care, I will spill your wine-cup. Rather
would I lose half my lands than separate from Agnes
my wife." The bishop of Paris was robbed of all his
goods, and the bishop of Senlis barely escaped with
his life. Philip had learnt from Henry II. how to
treat a recalcitrant priesthood. He himself remained
in Paris or within its diocese, in his new Norman
conquests, or in the diocese of Sens. It may be that
where he was not the dread sentence might be re-
laxed. He was himself not excommunicate. That
last terror the pope still held over his head ; and
his uncle of Rheims still stood by him. In September
he wrote to complain of the severity of the legate,
and he summoned the clergy and barons to consult
with him. Agnes appeared before them to excite their
compassion, but with one accord they told him that

he must put her away. "Is it true," said Philip to
his uncle, the metropolitan, "that the pope has declared your sentence of divorce to be but a farce?"
The archbishop was silent. "Then you are a fool
and madman to have pronounced it," cried the king.
Again he appealed to Rome, and Agnes pleaded for
her youth, her children, her innocent intent. At last
it seemed that the long strife might end. Every
one had turned against the king, and when the pope
sent, with another legate, cardinal Octavian of Ostia, a
kinsman of the king, it was seen that all that was
possible would be done to smooth the way for submission.
The king met the legates with respect. Their in-
structions were clear that he must abandon the wife he
had illegally taken, restore those he had dispossessed,
make reparation, receive back Ingeborgis. If this were
done, then might the question of divorce be thoroughly
sifted, in the presence of envoys of the Danish king
and with all legal forms. On September 7, 1200, a
great assembly met at the castle of S. Leger, near
Rambouillet. Ingeborgis herself lay there. An immense
crowd assembled, and watched, with keenest anxiety,
for the news of what was happening within. For a
time Philip held out; then with the two legates he
went to his injured wife, for the first time since the
hasty visit in the convent. "The pope does me violence,"
he said. She replied quietly, "No, he wills only that
justice should triumph." Then they led her before
the council, and Philip promised before all again to
take her to him. The bells pealed out, and the interdict
was at an end.

Even yet Philip had not fully yielded. He would

not let Ingeborgis live with him.   He declared that
she was his kinswoman, and he looked for the council
that had been promised to grant him a formal divorce.
Agnes was put away, and she bore him, a few weeks
later, a child whom Philip named after himself.   Six
months, six weeks, six days, and a council met at
Soissons to decide the question.   Meanwhile Ingeborgis received, so the legate informed Innocent, all
the honours of a queen, but she was strictly confined
to the castle of Étampes, and no one was allowed to
see her without the king's special permission.   Philip
left no stone unturned to influence the Roman Curia
in favour of a divorce.   It was then that the supple
chaplain, William the Breton, paid so many visits to
Rome that his friend, Giles of Paris, the poet, said,
"These are not journeys that you take : you live at
Rome."   In the register of Philip Augustus there
exists a curious list of the cardinals, with notes of those
who support the king, drawn up, it may be, at a later
date, but showing how carefully Philip's agents worked
in the Lateran.   Octavian, it seemed, had been won
over by his kinsman, the king.   The queen herself
complained of his attitude.   Innocent, however, remained firm.   He wrote letters consoling Ingeborgis,
and pointing out how much had already been won, and
he advised the Danish king of the coming council.   To
Octavian he wrote with decision.   It was his duty to
urge the king to take back Ingeborgis as his wife.   To
Philip he wrote, "There is no question of violence in
this submission, but only of right and of the salutary
treatment of the soul.   We would exhort you in friendly
fashion to take again the queen.   No one is more highly

placed by birth; she is not only pure but even a saint, by general confession. It is always your duty to fulfil the commands that the Apostolic See has for a long time laid upon you, for they are serious. If these commands are not fulfilled, you will give to the other side a pretext to refuse an answer on the question of right."

This was not all. The bishops who had not obeyed the interdict had been suspended by the legate, and were now summoned to Rome. There they were treated with severity, but eventually absolved. Hugh of Auxerre was not allowed to receive the archbishopric of Sens, the "wages of his iniquity." "My lord of Auxerre shall sing true, henceforth," said a wit, "yet shall he not gain so much as he lost by singing false." It is indeed amazing to count the threads which Innocent held in his hands in the autumn of 1201. Almost every European sovereign was in direct relations on some important matter with the Lateran, the difficulties between France and England were in a critical condition, and still the pope was pressing on a crusade with all the ardour of an unquenchable enthusiasm.

On March 2, 1201, the council met at Soissons. King and queen were both present. The Danish envoys, with the archbishop of Lund himself, urged the cause of their king's unhappy sister. Philip was surrounded by a host of lawyers. The training which provided him with diplomatists and administrators should serve him now in a matter which he had so near at heart. He claimed the dissolution of the marriage on the ground of kinship. The Danish envoys replied by urging that Philip had taken solemn oath to wed the lady : they declared that he was false and perjured, that Octavian, his kinsman, was no fair judge, that at Rome alone should the cause be heard, and, refusing to make further plaint, they returned to their own land before the legate John, cardinal of S. Paul, to whom also the hearing of the suit was assigned, had arrived at Soissons.

Nevertheless, on the second legate's appearance the council proceeded. For a fortnight the discussion continued. The English chronicler who tells of the council relates that an unknown priest of marvellous eloquence, learning, and modesty, pleaded the cause òf Ingeborgis, and when he had done left the hall never to be seen again. Marvellous though the incidents of the trial may have been, more marvellous was its close. Philip suddenly "wearied," says Rigord, "by the long delay, leaving the cardinals and bishops without even salutation, early in the morn departed with Ingeborgis, his wife, informing the court through his messengers that he took away his wife with him as his own and would not be separated from her." And he rode from the town with his wife behind him on the saddle. Well might Innocent have called the end of this amazing marriage question, as he had called the divorce, "ludibrii fabula."

The council broke up. There was no cause before it. Octavian remained in France. John returned to Italy. No sentence had been pronounced, and Philip could, if he would, cast the whole matter again into contest. That this was his intention he made clear by a letter which he at once sent to the pope. In this he recorded the opening of the council, the departure of the Danish envoys, the prolongation of the cause from day to day.

" We, therefore, seeing the vain delays and our manifest prejudice which should come through the sentence of your legates, departed thence, seeing only that they in no wise intended to end our suit." That the suit should be heard again and brought to prompt conclusion without the intervention of witnesses whom Ingeborgis demanded, he now claimed. If this should be, then he would again appear. If not, he would no longer try the suit. He ended by asking for the legitimation of the children whom Agnes had borne.

A few months later Agnes herself died—on July 19, or 20, 1201—at the Castle of Poissy. Her lover buried her at Mantes in the Church of S. Corentin, where he founded later a Benedictine nunnery. At the end of the year Innocent issued letters legitimising her children. The son was declared capable of succeeding to the throne. It was an act, as it seemed, of justice. The second marriage itself was annulled. It was illegal and contrary to the moral principles of the Church. But a sentence of nullity of the first marriage, invalid though it was, had been pronounced by the French bishops, and on the faith of it Agnes, and even Philip, might lawfully have wedded. The pope condemned sin, he did not punish the innocent. Early in 1202 the legitimation was publicly declared by all the French bishops. Already a marriage ·had been arranged for the little Philip with the baby daughter of Reginald of Boulogne. The first act of Philip's tragic wedding had ended.

The Frankish king could now turn again to his German and English negotiations. Again he besought Innocent to condemn Otto's cause and to support the

new candidate; again he drew closer the bonds that
linked him with Rome against the Angevins. In the
north Cnut VI. had warmly espoused the cause of Otto.
He had married his sister to William, Otto's brother,
whom some had thought of as heir to the English crown.
The cause of the Saxon Emperor seemed bright.

The marriage with Ingeborgis did not long remain
in the background. Philip, it seems, had never really
taken her back as his wife. When he had won his
way as to the legitimation of his children he again
besieged the ears of Innocent with cries for the dissolution of his marriage. Louis his father, the Emperor
Frederic, John of England himself within the last
few years, had had their causes tried by bishops of
their own. Why should he not have the same course
open? Innocent replied with dignity that in the case
of the emperor a legate had been present, that in the
two other cases the suit was unopposed. He declared
that he would hear the case himself, with all fit witnesses and documents that might be presented. The
delays, he repeated, were of Philip's making. Had he
from the first acted honestly the suit would have been
ended long ago. Let him learn how much was lost by
too much haste. By letter after letter he insisted on the
proper treatment of Ingeborgis. She lived a solitary life
under the strictest guard. It was said that no priest
was ever allowed to approach her, and that she could
rarely hear mass. She was left almost without clothes,
quite without the common decencies of life. Her
piteous letters but rarely reached the Lateran, and
when Innocent was aware of her condition he could do
no more than appeal to the king's honour, and finally

instruct the abbat of Casamari, his new legate, to enforce the redress of her wrongs. For years the political difficulties prevented any settlement. Ingeborgis suffered : Innocent entreated and threatened : but Philip remained obstinate, and gradually the French barons formed a strong party around him to resist the aggression of the Holy See. Philip in 1205 tried a new plea. He declared that he was bewitched—that he could not approach his wife. Sorcery was at work ; only the dissolution of the marriage could save him. Grotesquely this strange tale runs through the negotiations between papal legates and the French and English kings. Innocent was compelled to give it, contemptuously, some attention. But he utterly failed to bring the whole matter any nearer to a final conclusion. Philip would have nothing to say to Ingeborgis, and in other directions he was solacing himself by less legitimate unions, which continued for some years. Of one of these was born the young "Karlotides," whom the author of the Philippid eulogises.

Philip indeed felt himself at ease and his throne secure. He had two sons recognised as legitimate. He had many means of keeping the pope at arm's length. In 1207 Innocent besought him to live with Ingeborgis as his wife, or if that were impossible at least to allow her the state and dignity of queen. Philip sent the abbat of S. Geneviève to Rome to press on the business of the divorce, and to urge that his reunion with his wife should not be regarded as a barrier to it. " Far from it : " wrote Innocent, " if you desire to break the charm you should approach reunion with your wife with prayer, alms, the offering of the Holy Sacrifice, with fear of God and with faith." Still the stories of sorcery grew. A priest declared that he had seen the devil sitting on the queen's knees. Women added curious details to the scandal. Every one talked of the king's business, and Philip was sardonically immovable and content.

He was indeed now able to put off the too-pressing solicitations of the pope by changing the subject to one which seemed even more near to the interests of the Church. Already the crimes and heresies of Southern Gaul cried urgently for the intervention of Rome. In the early summer of 1208 Innocent sent the cardinal deacon Guala to France, a man "learned in the law and ornate with good manners," to urge the king to undertake a crusade against the Albigenses. He was charged at the same time to investigate the question of sorcery, and if there should prove to be such an impediment to pronounce the dissolution of the marriage. Philip was not even yet put to his last shift. He induced Ingeborgis to retire to a convent, and he now declared that the marriage must be dissolved because she had taken monastic vows. Innocent again repeated the occasions under which a divorce by canon law might be possible, but absolutely refused to pronounce a dissolution of the marriage without a full investigation. "Meanwhile," he declared, "you must give freedom to the queen, so that she may be free to consult with her kin, may have no violence to fear, and may prepare herself as she thinks fit for the trial." The king himself should be instructed by men learned in the law that the pope decreed nothing anew, but was acting entirely in accordance with the rules of canon law. No sooner was power given to Guala to hold inquest in the matter than Philip declared that the delay was intolerable. A brief letter which he sent to the legate at the beginning of 1209 is worth quotation in full.

"Philip, by the grace of God, King of the Franks, to his beloved Guala, cardinal deacon of S. Mary in Porticu and legate of the apostolic see, salutation and sincere goodwill. Your goodwill is aware that our clerk whom we sent to the apostolic see is returned. The lord pope puts so many matters and so many delays in our business, that, as it seems to us, he does not will to liberate us, as we need, at once. Wherefore, since it is evident to us that he will not liberate us as it is expedient for us, we command that, concerning that matter, unless you have anything that may be done, you shall make no further stay in this land."

So the affair dragged on. Innocent wrote to Philip that the glory of his great conquests was dimmed by his conduct to his queen. To Ingeborgis he wrote of the consolations of religion. "As by marriage you are called to rule over others, be you also mistress of yourself, in that strife whereby God would prove your virtue. Support yourself in all your suffering with a contrite spirit, not only with submission but with glad acceptance of the Divine Will. Your Father would prove you as fathers of this world prove their children, who bring them up not in pleasures but in hardness."

Philip meanwhile was knitting closer his political alliance with the Holy See. He was at least friendly to the Albigensian war. He was summoning his bishops to send men to aid the pope in his struggle with Otto. He was still discussing unsavoury details

with the pope and his envoys. He was still crying out
for a dissolution of his unhappy marriage. He was
still keeping Ingeborgis in strict seclusion. But he was
preparing none the less surely to submit to a reunion if
it should confirm by a strong alliance the basis of his
political power in Europe. In November 1210 he
promised to marry the daughter of Hermann, landgrave
of Thuringia, if he could make the pope pronounce a
divorce. But in 1213, on the point of the invasion of
England, when he was trying to gather round him
every possible ally to ward off the danger of the great
coalition that was ready to press on him suddenly—
very likely by the advice of Guèrin, his near friend and
chief counsellor, the famous warrior-statesman and clerk
—he took again his banished queen, "from whom," says
William the Breton (discreetly silent year by year as
to the earlier troubles) "he had separated now for
sixteen years and more," and there was great joy among
the people.

This act, in spite of elaborate historical investigations
of French and German students, remains little easier to
explain than Philip's long stubbornness or his first disgust.
The alliance of Denmark and its fleet, the blessing of
Innocent, the re-habilitation of his character in the eyes
of the French church and the people, these had suddenly
assumed a new worth in Philip's eyes. He may well
have wished to provide himself with a new ally at
the moment when John (13th May 1213) made peace
with the pope, and to win the pope's protection at a
time when he seemed to be likely to throw all his
weight on to the side of the coalition against France.
And in the results of his act he was not disappointed.

From that day, though dangers closed around him, he
rode triumphantly through.   The victory of Bouvines
men took to be the Divine reward for the restoration of
the injured queen.   From this time Ingeborgis resumed
her constitutional rights as Frankish queen.   Charters
record her sanction, and the king himself confirms her
will in 1218 and promises benefactions in her memory.
She outlived him, still exercising royal dignities, and
died at last in July 1236.   The long struggle cannot
be said to mark any striking triumph of either king or
pope.   The dogged obstinacy which lay behind Philip's
hot passions comes out in his persistent and determined
resistance to the voice of authority propounding the
law of Christian morals.   His ingenuity and cunning
are no less evident, and equally so the width of his interests and his grasp of political combinations over a
wide field.   It is difficult in a short survey to give
any idea of the complications of European policy with
which the marriage question was involved.   The effects
of political changes on the action of Philip on the one
hand and of Innocent on the other may, it is true, be
easily exaggerated.   The changes cannot be traced with
anything like the same certainty as can those which the
successes or reverses of Frederic I. caused in the attitude of Alexander III. to Henry II. and Becket.
Innocent was a very different man from Alexander.
His letters can be read without the detection of any
weakness or enforced change of policy.   He was per-
fectly clear all through in his willingness to investigate,
in a lawful manner, any reason that might be alleged
for the dissolution of the marriage, equally clear in his
assertion of the moral claims of the wife and the moral

duties of the husband. So far as it was possible to succeed he succeeded. He enforced the withdrawal of the illegal and dishonest divorce. He compelled Philip to put away Agnes. He compelled him again to recognise Ingeborgis as his lawful wife. But not even a pope could compel a man to live with his wife or to give her more than the necessaries of life. He could remonstrate and even threaten, but there was a point at which the legal sanction of the church definitely ceased. Innocent went as far as he was justified in going, but not an inch beyond. Philip for a long time set decency and good feeling at defiance, but Innocent by his persistence, his moderation, and the moral earnestness of his denunciations, turned against the French king the whole feeling of his people and of Europe, and in the end won by patience far more than he would have been able to secure by anathema.

While Innocent was drawn in one direction by his moral objections to Philip, he was drawn the opposite way by the necessities of the church in Southern Gaul. There the reconquest of the people by the church tended inevitably to become the conquest of the land by the French crown.

The end of the twelfth century and the beginning of the thirteenth, a period of great intellectual activity over a somewhat narrow field of investigation, was of necessity a period of widespread intellectual revolt against the doctrinal system of the church. Philosophy studied in distortion, and theology apprehended in a mist of words, naturally produced heresy, and heresy produced rebellion. The history of the early church repeated itself in the Gaul of the Middle Ages. Individuals, inspired by a genuine desire to repress abuses and to restore a "primitive" or "pure" Christian faith, put their theories into practice, found them exaggerated by disciples, and eventually were carried away by the excesses of mobs who made any relaxation of the old discipline an opportunity for the wildest moral divergence. The age of Philip Augustus was an age of Sectarianism in France.

As a rule throughout Europe the only opposition which the Christian faith had met for centuries was that presented by the rigid and from time to time aggressive attitude of Judaism. Towards the ancient people Philip's relations were changeable, selfish, and treacherous. He found them in possession of a reasonable security, with synagogues, liberties, and State recognition. One of his first acts was to reverse the toleration of his father. On a Sabbath in March 1180, says Rigord, "all the Jews throughout France were taken in their synagogues and then spoiled of their gold and silver and raiment, as the Jews themselves spoiled the Egyptians at the Exodus." Not content with this Philip carried out a further "spoiling" a few months later. He declared all debts to the Jews null and void, taking to himself a fifth part of each debt which he released his subjects from paying. This honest proceeding did not satisfy either king or people. In April 1182 Philip issued an edict that all Jews should depart from the realm before midsummer day. They were allowed to sell their property—a marvellous generosity, thinks Rigord; and by the end of July they had left the land. To pass in 1182 over the borders of France into the dominions of Henry II. was a hardship which we might

easily exaggerate ; and it is clear from later evidence
that the expulsion was not complete. In 1192 Philip
himself burnt eighty of them at Brie-Comte-Robert on
suspicion of the murder of a Christian, a barbarity such
as he delighted in. In 1197 he gave license to Jews to
return to his lands, and the edicts of the later years of
his reign contain many instances of regulations concerning them. In 1204 we find several lists of Jews
suffered to remain in the land, with the amount of their
pledges. The names show that they had dwelt in
different parts of the country, from Normandy to
Orleans, Étampes, Senlis, and Bourges. He entered also
into the negotiations by which his great vassals suffered
Jews to dwell in their lands, and in 1219 he issued a
special établissement defining their rights and securing
their position, which may be compared with the Statute
de Judaismo of Edward I.

Till the end of the thirteenth century it might seem
to readers of the French chronicles as if the Jews were
the only dissenters with whom the king and the church
had to reckon. A little further investigation shows how
deceptive would be such an impression. Already old
sects were revived, new sects originated, all over Gaul,
and, in the south, organised bodies had sprung into
vigorous life and threatened the dominance and even
the very existence of the church. It is easy to throw
the blame for the subsequent excesses upon the sloth of
the church and the luxury of the clergy, and to find in
the Troubadours' songs ample evidence of the urgent need
for reform. "The cupidity, dissimulation, and baseness
of the clergy," says Sismondi, "had rendered them odious
to the nobles and the people." "The black monks are

unrivalled in their eating and their loves; the white
monks in their lies; the knights of Temple and Hospital
in their pride, and the canons in usury," sang a minstrel
of the south. "They love the fair lady and the red
wine," said another. It is ill to seek evidence against
any class from popular songs or dramas, but there is
not wanting proof to substantiate, with some modifications, the charges which the Troubadours bring against
the church for its corruptions. The higher clergy, the
great prelates, lived, there can be no doubt, lives of
ease and luxury. They were gentlemen and politicians
before they were priests and preachers. And the clergy
were, at the least, not equal to dealing with the intellectual and moral difficulties which led to the recru-
descence of old heresies.

At the close of the twelfth century individual heretics
and freethinkers, the founders of new schools and the
knight-errants of unpopular opinions, Berengar of Tours,
Abailard, Arnold of Brescia, had given way to organised
bodies whose origin or founder it is not easy to trace,
whose tenets were of every shade of divergence, but
who all agreed in opposition to the church. Comparing
this epoch with the days of the early church it has been
pointed out that the different sects fall into three classes,
which follow the old lines of the Montanists, Pantheists,
and Manicheans.

To the first class belong the followers of Peter of
Bruys, who at the beginning of the century had in the
south of France opposed baptism, celibacy, and the
church's doctrines of the ministry, the Real Presence and
the Sacrifice in the mass. He was himself burnt in
1124 : of his followers some were converted by a mission

of S. Bernard, some lingered till 1184, when they united with the Waldenses or followers of Peter Waldo (or Valdez). This man had given himself to the task of evangelising the south by the same methods of poverty and penance. It is difficult to recover his actual teaching, but it would appear to have included a rejection of all the sacraments save the Eucharist, and of the ministry. His society, which continued after the founder's excommunication in 1184, is represented—though not by an exact succession—to this day in Dauphiny and Piedmont. Its influence in the thirteenth century was not great.

Amaury, a logician of Paris, gave an impetus at the end of the twelfth century to the Pantheism which has always remained on the fringe of Christian teaching, by proclaiming the incarnation of the Holy Spirit in every Christian. From this he proceeded to the deduction that sacraments were useless, and that the sole qualification for a holy life was the knowledge of the presence of God. His opinions, condemned by Innocent III. and retracted by himself, had much weight for some time. The chroniclers record several condemnations and several executions of the Amauricians, as his followers were called, but the body remained rather intellectually than numerically a danger to the church.

The fascinating Manicheism which all through the Middle Ages cast its glamour over many races of Southern Europe sprang into new life in the twelfth century. The heretics of Southern Gaul, Albigenses as they came to be called, were almost entirely Manichean. Kathari, Paulicians, Bulgarians, many different names the chroniclers find for them, but their teaching, it is clear, is similar to that of the Manicheism which died so hard in its struggle with the early church. The leading principle was dualism, and a declaration of the eternity of the evil and the good in perpetual antagonism. The church historians of the age delight to dwell upon the extraordinary beliefs which they discovered in those they questioned—the contrast between the true God, the author of the New Testament, and Jehovah the evil spirit, the author of the Old Testament, whose son Lucifer had led astray a number of the angels and imprisoned them in earthly bodies, whom Christ, another angel, had descended from heaven to redeem. In some of its tenets that Catharism of the south resembled the bitter Calvinism which was later to represent another reaction against the teaching of the church in France. It distinguished men into two classes, of which one only could come to salvation. Just as these ideas struck at the root of all morality, being, like Calvinism, not accidentally but essentially immoral, so the repudiation by the Cathari of all church order, of marriage, and of property struck at all the foundations of society as well as the bases of the church.

The system of the Albigenses in fact was "not only a religious but also a social heresy, and this explains in part the severity with which it was suppressed." Appearing in different places in the eleventh century, in the twelfth the new teaching spread itself over Southern Gaul. It met the stream of Vaudois or Waldensian influence but formed no union with it. The two systems agreed only in opposition to the church. By the end of the twelfth century the Cathari had taken the district of Albi for their centre, whence came the name of Albigenses which was soon applied to them, and had acquired the support and protection of a large number of the nobles of the district, chief of whom was the head of the great house of Toulouse, Raymond VI. of S. Gilles.

The south, open to every subtle influence of disintegration which the Italian disturbances of the age so readily furnished, full of wild superstition, wild luxury, wilder enthusiasms and licence than Northern France could foster, eagerly accepted the growth of secret societies, which the lords encouraged as a counterpoise to the riches and the power of the church. Provence, the region between the Haute Garonne, the Cévennes, the Isère, the Alps and the sea, became almost wholly given over to the Albigensian teaching. The extreme licence of manners which had long marked the South welcomed the new theories of religion, which in reality gave a basis for a new morality. Jews and Mussalmans had already accustomed the people to revolt from the church system. An intoxication, as from new wine, overspread the land. "Le midi," says Michelet in his picturesque way, "délirait à la veille de sa ruine." Raymond V. had called in the French and English kings to suppress heresy. When Raymond VI. threw himself heartily into the revolution, Toulouse became the capital of the heretical kingdom. Southern Gaul was trying to cut itself off from the church and from the Frankish suzerainty. It was an attempt at a political and religious revolution after the fashion of that which the sixteenth century was to see carried to a successful conclusion.

So little did the north know of the south, so common were attacks upon ecclesiastical property, and so familiar

the excesses of freebooting barons, that it was long
before the news spread, or was understood, that in
Provence bishops were being driven from their sees,
abbats from their monasteries, priests from their livings.
The wandering bands of discharged soldiers and trucu-
lent knights who plundered the north, joined hands
in the south with the heretics, and the whole country
was given over to licence and confusion. The church
gradually awoke to the danger. Alexander III. and the
Third Lateran Council condemned the new teachers and
ordered drastic measures for their suppression. More
strongly Lucius III. at Verona in 1184 laid under
perpetual anathema "the Cathari and Paterines, those
who call themselves poor men of Lyons (the followers
of Peter Waldo), the Passagines, Josephines, and
Arnaldists." Bishops were ordered to send commissions of inquest into the districts where heresy
existed, and to deliver the city to the secular power.
Innocent III. took up the work in earnest. In 1198
he sent two Cistercians to preach in the south, with
commission from him as his legates. He added later
Pierre of Castelnau, archdeacon of Maguelonne, Cardinal
Raoul and the abbat of Citeaux, Arnauld Amaury.
The last was a great preacher, and he was joined by a
greater, the mighty S. Dominic himself. For ten years
the Spanish saint walked over the whole land, heedless
of the tumult and war which surrounded him. His
efforts at the time seemed to have met with only the
very smallest success. Arnauld's preaching had no
better result. "This holy man," says the Troubadour,
"went out with others over the land of the heretics,
preaching to them that they should be converted, but

the more he besought them the more they scoffed
at him and held him for a fool." For four years
Peter of Castelnau held on his way. Negligent and
worldly bishops were deposed, immoral clerks degraded, reformation was taken in hand sternly and
without respect of persons. But reformation did not
check the disorder which it was to the interest of the
great lords to foster. In 1207 Peter determined to
compel the mighty count of Toulouse to restore the
churches which he had seized. Raymond refused and
was excommunicated. Filled with rage he vowed
vengeance on the insolent clerk. One of his knights
pursued the legate, and at S. Gilles, near Arles, in
January 1208 he stabbed him to the heart.

The murder of Peter of Castelnau was the signal
for the outbreak of war. Innocent, who had watched
the beginnings of the strife with calm restraint, now
stretched out his hand like an avenging angel. The
whirlwind and the storm passed over the unhappy land
of Languedoc, and it was the pope who rode triumphant,
directing the thunder where to strike. He immediately
excommunicated the count of Toulouse, released his
subjects from their fealty, placed his lands under
interdict, and offered them to the first who should
seize them from the heretic's hand. He sent Guala to
Philip to implore his aid, and he wrote to the king and
all the chief lords of the land, "commanding and
directing that as catholic and faithful servants of Jesus
Christ they should invade with a mighty army the
lands of Toulouse and Albi, of Quercy and Narbonne
and Béziers, and should utterly destroy all the heretics
who possessed those lands."

With this declaration, and the pope's promise of absolution to those who died in the war, Rigord's chronicle concludes. The conclusion comes fitly at the beginning of a new epoch in the history of Southern Gaul. It was a new Crusade which Innocent preached. Its execution involved an entire reconstruction of the political system of the south. Beginning by fighting for their lawlessness of opinion and of life, for their liberty to kill and devour one another after the fashion of unchecked feudal independence, the people of Languedoc came gradually to fight for their local customs, laws, and language, for their historical severance from the north, for their autonomy against the advancing sovereignty of the Frankish king. Innocent began the work of conversion to the Church. The process which he inaugurated ended by giving to the Capets the sovereignty of an united France. The Albigensian crusade went far to complete what the fall of the Angevins had begun.

In a few months a mighty army assembled in answer to the pope's appeal. Barons of the north and centre, some great lords and bishops even of the south, swelled the ranks of the army of the Church. The duke of Burgundy, the counts of Nevers and Auxerre, Gaucher de Châtillon, count of S. Pol, who was so greatly to distinguish himself at Bouvines, and Simon de Montfort, count of Evreux, were among the great leaders who brought their forces to the war. Innocent expressly reserved the rights of the suzerain when he directed this overpowering force upon the lands of the heretical and profligate count of Toulouse. He foresaw, there can be no doubt, the end of the great crusade.

Philip himself was invited to take command of the host. "Rise," cried Innocent, "rise, most Christian king. Hear the cry of blood. Help to take on the sinners the vengeance of blood." But Philip was far too much occupied with danger more near at hand—with Otto and John, with the treachery of his own border vassals, with fears of a wider attack. He had at his sides two great and terrible lions, he said. He was quite ready to see his work done by the army of the crusade.

Simon de Montfort took command of the host. Raymond, adulterer, wrapped in luxury, and long the supporter of heretics because they laid no severe restraints on his way of living, awoke to find destruction at his doors. He appealed to Philip, who refused to interfere. He appealed to the Emperor Otto, of whom he held Provence. Lastly, he appealed to Innocent himself, and at length made a complete submission. On June 18, 1209, having vowed to extirpate heresy, and to restore the wronged, having given up seven castles as security and submitted to open penance, Raymond himself took the cross. But his submission did not check the campaign. His nephew and vassal, Raymond Roger, viscount of Carcassonne and Béziers, stood out against every threat. The army of Simon de Montfort carried all before it; Béziers was stormed, Carcassonne fell, the viscount was cast into a dungeon, and died, men said of poison, on November 10. The lands that had been conquered were offered to the duke of Burgundy, to the count of S. Pol, and the count of Nevers. They refused the dangerous honour, and Simon de Montfort was invested with the forfeited districts. The establishment of a northern baron in the southern fief turned

the war of religion into a war of persons and of race.
He had fought for the faith, men said, but he had
conquered for himself.   The people rose against him
as the crusaders retired to their own estates, and, in
1210, of all the castles he had won Simon de Montfort
held but eight.   The war began afresh : the crusade
was over.   Raymond of Toulouse found the conditions
to which he had agreed to be irksome in the extreme.
The legates excommunicated him anew.   Again he
appealed to Philip, who remained silent.   He appealed
to the pope, who referred him to a council which should
assemble at S. Gilles.   He obtained some delay.   In
February 1211 he appeared before the legates at Arles,
where the terms offered him were such as he would not
accept.   He determined on a last stand.   He threw himself into Toulouse, and his people promised to stand by
him to the death.   A new crusade began with his resistance.   He had definitely, on whatever provocation, thrown
his weight against the Church and the army of the north.
He was now to feel their overwhelming superiority.   A
real conquest of the south began.   As town by town
was taken, heresy was searched for and stamped out.
Each fief won was given to knights of the northern
land, and Church possessions as well as baronies were
conferred on members of the crusading force.   The
abbat of Citeaux became archbishop of Narbonne and
took the title of duke.   Folquet, to whom the legates
had years before given the see of Toulouse, himself a
Marseillais and a Troubadour, who appears in the third
heaven of the *Paradiso* among the blessed spirits who
had resigned an earthly for a heavenly love, welcomed
the northern forces with open arms.

The crusade for a time appeared to be checked, when Pedro II. of Aragon, the gallant champion of his own land against the infidel, interceded for the unhappy land of Languedoc, and obtained from Innocent, who had certainly no motives but the highest in his aims for the reformation of the south, a temporary suspension of operations. But the legates were not to finish their work, and Simon de Montfort saw in the war the opportunity of bringing a larger district under his sway. The council of Lavaur (1213), it was hoped, might bring peace, but Raymond's attitude as a supporter of heresy was so clear that it ended only in his renewed excommunication. As the crusaders won inch by inch from the great count of Toulouse, Pedro of Aragon saw a new reason for intervention. The southern border lands, over which he had exercised a semi-suzerainty, and which had stood as a protection between himself and the aggressive powers of the north, were slowly being absorbed into the great kingdom of the Capets. He determined to make a stand for their independence. He marched troops into the county of Toulouse. On September 12, 1213, was fought the great battle of Muret, one of the most decisive events in the history of Southern Gaul. The king of Aragon was killed, and his army was totally routed. The victory, in which the French king was in no way concerned, was almost as important a step in the establishment of his power as the battle of Bouvines or his triumphs over Henry II. and John. It decided once for all that Languedoc should pass under the control of the north; and the power of the north meant inevitably, and at no long distance of time, the power of the Capetian house.

Raymond VI. submitted immediately after the battle. The consuls of Toulouse handed over their city to the crusaders. At a council held at Montpellier, January 8, 1215, Simon de Montfort was chosen lord of the whole land. Thus the ancient house of Toulouse, which, in spite of its nominal vassalage, had long treated on equal terms with the French kings, was completely crushed. Every new power that came into existence in the thirteenth century was compelled to recognise from the first the position which the Frank monarchy had won. Simon de Montfort became count of Toulouse, duke of Narbonne, viscount of Carcassonne. Raymond VII., son of the unhappy count who had lost all, received the marquisate of Provence.

The crusade was over, but a dynastic war remained. The young Raymond, himself a Catholic and favoured by the pope, determined to win back the heritage of his fathers. Battle after battle again desolated the country. Raymond VI. appeared from his hiding, captured Foix, and held it against his foes. The death of Simon de Montfort, June 25, 1218, seemed to throw success once more into the hands of the men of the south, and a desultory warfare did little to establish the claims of Amaury, the son of the great crusader.

Now, at length, Philip thought that the time had come to secure for himself the fruits that had been won for him by others. Yet still he would not listen to the urgent appeals of Honorius III. to intervene in person. The chroniclers at this point are almost silent. A crusade, the last work of the greatest of medieval popes, was diverting the energies of many in France. The king was feeling at length secure upon his throne. Yet even now he would not risk an insurrection by absence from the centre of his power. His son, the young Louis, had already tried a knight-errant scheme of winning England for the French. In the south he was more likely to achieve success. On Ascension Day 1219, "sent by his father," as William the Breton assures us, Louis, with Peter Mauclerc the Breton duke, the bishops of Noyon, Senlis, and Tournai, one at least of whom had shown his valour in the field, and a host of other bishops, earls, and barons, and a vast multitude of knights and foot-men, set forward to the conquest of the south. The expedition, ending with a long siege of Toulouse, was a complete failure. Amaury de Montfort endeavoured to induce Philip to take up the cause himself, and to receive as his own all that the Church had given to Simon; and Conrad of Porto, the pope's legate, and four of the southern bishops strongly urged him to accept the offer. In nothing did the great king show his wisdom more clearly than by his refusal. He had not lost by the failure of the expedition: he was not going by precipitation to mar the work that time would inevitably do for his house.

His sagacity had rightly foreseen the end of the strife. He died himself before Languedoc became an actual part of the French king's direct domain. But in 1224 Amaury de Montfort ceded his rights to the French king, and in 1229 Blanche of Castile, widow of Louis VIII., made the treaty of Meaux, by which the crown received immediate possession of the territory between the Rhone and Narbonne, and was promised

after the death of Raymond VII. the whole county of
Toulouse.

Long before the southern fiefs were actually united
to the French king's domains, northern influence had
permeated the land, the national literature had sunk
into decay, the *langue d'oc* had yielded to the tongue
of the north, and the Church had re-established her sway.
A bloody war, a long and patient mission of preaching
friars, a slow growth of northern influence, had made
Southern Gaul recognise that it was one land with the
kingdom which had held the emperor at bay and
triumphed over the great house of Anjou.

Philip's attitude during the whole duration of the
war is worthy of careful attention. His policy, as in
the difficulties of his marriage, was one of masterly
inactivity. Within his own domain he would sternly
suppress heretical teaching. He was a bitter foe to
heretics. William the Breton records with pride how
in 1183 he purged his land of "Popelicani" (publicani,
a Manichean sect which had appeared in France in
1175), by condemning them to the flames; and the
Couteraux, of whom he is said to have slain seven
thousand in Berry in the same year, fell also under
the condemnation of the Church. In December 1207
he gave formal answer through the bishop of Paris
to the demands of Innocent III. for help. He stated
that John was already laying siege to the castle of
Belleville, belonging to his vassal de Mauléon, and that
it was necessary for him to go to its aid. He could
not have two armies in the field at once, one to fight
the Albigenses, one to protect his own territories. But
if the pope would make a truce between John and

himself, then he would willingly assist the crusaders. It is a typical document. Equally characteristic is the letter addressed at the end of 1218 to Thibault, count of Champagne, warning him that his intervention in Toulouse must not prejudice his duty to serve the king in his wars with England. Carlyle might have said of him, as he said of the great Elector, that, if he "advanced in circles," he had "his reasonable private aim sun clear all the time."

Philip's greatness is seen in nothing more clearly than in his patience, and this characteristic is revealed in the clearest light by his conduct towards the Albigensian crusade. It might have seemed that by active intervention he would have secured the pope's favour, and added, without the cost of many men or much money, a vast province to the direct dominions of the crown. But he saw clearly that the complication of religious and political ends in the crusade would have been to his own prospects not a strength but a weakness. He saw that the Church must conquer, and that her conquest meant the victory of the north. He knew that, when the spoils came to be divided, no power could step in to claim against the Frankish king the lion's share.

Philip's relations with the papacy illustrate his extraordinary acuteness of vision and his indomitable obstinacy and patience. He carried through legislation, such as had well-nigh cost the greatest of the Angevins his crown, and such as Henry II. had been compelled with the most humiliating submission to withdraw. He held out against the head of the Catholic world on a moral question with a diplomacy which kept the papal curia itself at bay. And, without taking part in a crusade which lay near to the heart of the great ruler of the Church, he managed not to incur his censure, and eventually reaped all the rewards of the expedition.

CHAPTER VII

LAST YEARS

THE victory of Bouvines was the culminating point of the great king's reign. In his later years, still vigilant and attent, he had chiefly to retain what he had already won.

At home he was able to rest upon his laurels. In 1215 he founded the abbey of Notre Dame de la Victoire, and he watched the preaching of a crusade on which Innocent III. had set his heart with cool indifference. "Robert de Corcon, the pope's legate," says William the Breton, "and many with him, preached publicly throughout all the realm in French, and gave the cross without distinction to many—children, old men, women, lame, blind, deaf, lepers; wherefore many rich men abhorred to take up the cross, because this confusion seemed like rather to hinder the crusade than to succour the Holy Land. But in their preachings, in which they seemed to wish to please the people more than is needful, they defamed the clergy, speaking and inventing base things before the people concerning their living, and so sowed matter of scandal and schism between clergy and people." Philip, it would seem, was himself at last

aroused. "For this cause, and for certain other •
grievances, the king and the whole clergy appealed to
the apostolic see against the legate."

Philip, now that his own business at Rome was over,
was not sorry, it may be, to have other cause of complaint. From such diversions, however, he was recalled
to more serious matters by the events which were
happening in England. John had offered—William the
Breton thinks—to buy back for an immense sum some
part of the lands he had lost. Philip had answered,
the story runs, with a bitter taunt. It was incredible
that one vowed to a crusade should have wished to buy
earthly possessions, or should have money to buy with.
For himself, he was rich, and ready to buy rather than
to sell lands. And to none would he part with, and
with none share, the territory he had received from his
fathers, or won with his sword. The story is incredible.
John was in no mood to make such an offer. He was
already tottering to his fall.

The events which followed John's repudiation of the
great Charter and his absolution by the pope turned
the eyes of Philip towards England, as well as those of
the English barons towards France. Philip was far
too astute to embroil himself in the affairs of England.
He could not, indeed, at this juncture enter into open
opposition to the pope. But the English barons were
not without hope of foreign aid. They found themselves, says Matthew Paris, placed in a most difficult
position, knowing that they could not trust John's
promises if they should make terms with him, and
having now both the pope and the king for their foes. But
taking counsel, they chose Louis, the eldest son of Philip

the king of the Franks, to be their king, which when
they announced both to the father and the son, King
Philip asked of them hostages and written pledges.
The barons, having no other refuge, gave what he
asked. No sooner was this known than Guala was sent
as legate from the pope to France that he might stay
the going of Louis by the authority of the apostolic
see. To Philip he brought letters of command that he
should not allow his son to go to England, or in any way
to vex the king of England, the vassal of the holy see.
Then, says the sturdy Englishman, King Philip straightway answered, "The kingdom of England never was
the patrimony of S. Peter, nor is, nor will be. No
king or prince can give away his realm, which is a
commonwealth, without the assent of his barons, who
are bound to defend the realm. And if the pope shall
have commanded this error he will set a pernicious
example to all kings and kingdoms. I do not love,
I do not regard John, king of the English, my rival,
yet still I grieve at his kingdom's servitude, when the
ruler of great provinces is laid under tribute. Alas !
how greatly will the state of all kings suffer through
this. So, by some trick, may the pope, in time to come,
rob my heir of France." Then raising his hands to
heaven he cried, "which may God, may God, may God
avert." Tears flowed from his eyes as he spoke ; and
his barons cried out that never should their land pass
by the mere will of king or prince into the power of
any pope or bishop or priest. And Louis spoke out
boldly. To his father and the legate he cried, "I beg
that you will not stay my will, for I will contend for
my heritage as long as my heart beats in my breast.

Base and brutish were it indeed to desert the barons of England, who fight for the freedom of their land and have chosen me to be their lord." And so in anger he departed, and King Philip declared that he would neither support nor hinder his going. On March 26, Louis threw himself at his father's feet and implored his permission to go, and his blessing on the expedition. Philip secretly gave him leave and blessed him. It must have been clear to all Europe that he approved the expedition, but he took no steps to support it. He watched the campaign with keen interest, but stood rigidly aloof. This did not satisfy Innocent III. He was now pledged to assist John as his own vassal. His threats induced Philip, if we may believe William the Breton, to declare all the lands of his son and the barons who had accompanied him forfeit to the crown. But in spite of this, Innocent sent letters threatening, if not actually pronouncing, the excommunication of the French king. Still Philip persevered in his neutral attitude. There is no sign of his interference till after John's death and Louis's defeat and the desertion of the barons, when an urgent appeal reached him for aid. "Is William the Marshal still alive?" he asked. And when he heard that he still lived, "Then is my son safe," he said; for he knew not that the Marshal had now gone over to the young Henry. He would not himself send aid, but left it to Blanche, his son's vigorous and devoted wife, to procure assistance. The utter defeat of the succours, and the capture and death of Eustace the Monk, made Louis's cause hopeless. Philip must have smiled grimly when he learnt that his son had pledged himself by treaty to urge the surrender to Henry of his rights oversea, and promised to restore them when he became king. If he had gained nothing by Louis's rash expedition, he had lost nothing in his own land.

With the war in the south he had little more concern. He invested Simon de Montfort with the county of Toulouse in 1216, but he would not actively intervene in the contest. His fighting days were over. He was reconciled to the Empire and the Papacy. England had sunk out of count in the affairs of Europe.

At home he saw the extinction of the old house of Chartres in 1218, and the division of Chartres and Blois between the counts of Beaumont and S. Pol, husbands of the last count's sisters. In Brittany, Peter Mauclerc, regent for his son, was engaged in many contests with the neighbouring lords, cleric and lay. In the next few years the whole interest of the country was engrossed in the Albigensian war, reopened by the young Raymond VII. Philip still held aloof. But in 1221, says a fragmentary continuation of one of the chroniclers, he sent two hundred knights to aid Amaury de Montfort. Year by year, at the pope's request, he renewed his truce with England. He had sheathed his sword. He felt that his work was done.

Here, before his eventful history ends, we may pause to see what was the place that he had won in his own land and among his contemporaries, and what manner of man was he whom his people called Augustus and Conqueror.

That Philip was ever greatly beloved, it would be difficult to prove. In his youth, at any rate, he was a stern man, in little sympathy with the coarse licentiousness and blasphemy of the times. "He loved justice," says Rigord, "as his own mother; he strove to exact mercy above judgment; he was ever a follower of the truth; he surpassed all other kings in conjugal chastity in his own house." In his court he would allow no profane oath. Even the oaths that men playing games of hazard or in taverns so often use, says the same worthy chronicler, he greatly abhorred; so that often, if a man by chance rapped out an oath, he would find himself of a sudden, by the royal order, thrown into the nearest river or pond, that he might cool his temper.

But as years went on, the king's virtues were not so apparent. His will so long uncontrolled would burst out into fury. He was relentless and cruel, yet there was a human touch about him that his father lacked. He rose to a great occasion. At Bouvines he appeared a real hero. And he won something of the popularity that always comes to a great conqueror. Some of the best lines in the twelve books of the *Philippid* are those when the poet, towards the close of his hero's life, speaks of the mutual affection of king and people.

> Pax erat in toto populis gratissima regno,
> Rexque gubernabat regnum populumque paterno
> Affectu, cunctos et amans et amatus ab illis,
> Nulli damnosus, nulli gravis, omnibus æquus,
> Omni præcipue cleri protector ab hoste;
> Sicque benignus erat, quod, amico pacis amicos
> Corde fovens, malefactores puniret acerbe.
> Unde vocabatur omni reverenter ab ore
> Cleri rex, patriæ pater, ecclesiæque columna.
> Nec sciri poterat mage diligat an populum rex,
> An regem populus; et erat contentio dulcis
> Inter eos super his, uter utri carior esset,
> Quem penes alterni vis esset major amoris,
> Tam puro nexu dilectio colligat ambos!

But William the Breton had some of the genius and all the vivid imagination of his race. To estimate the value of the praises of the great king, it is necessary to consider by whom they were sung.

What Philip really was, and what place he filled in the Europe of his day, is best seen when we observe the position of those who wrote of him. At home the great abbey of S. Denys, which had for so long trained statesmen and ecclesiastics, taught men to write as well as to rule. Here Suger himself had learnt to govern. His laxity had merited the stern rebukes of S. Bernard; he had taken the warning to heart and had reduced to order first his own monks and then the turbulent barons of the Frankish kingdom. He had told too the tale of the deeds of his schoolfellow and friend the great King Louis, deeds in the most famous of which he was himself a sharer. S. Denys was full of noble memories. Thither the kings came at all solemn times to pray, to sing Te Deum, to seek a sacred sanction for their wars or a pardon for their sins, to stand impressed and sobered by the sepulchres of the monarchs of their race. At S. Denys the monks watched eagerly, and carefully noted, what manner of men were those great kings who came among them so often. Courtiers coming and going told them the intrigues of the palace, statesmen and bishops spoke of the troubles of the time, monks bewailed the forays of greedy barons, and papal legates bore witness, sometimes to the avarice of the Roman court, sometimes to the far-sighted vigilance of the servant of the servants of God. There was little done in the land of the Franks that the monks of S. Denys did not hear of; and they had always a scribe ready to record, and copyists eager to spread abroad the history he had penned. Their chronicler was rarely a mere recluse : at the beginning of the thirteenth century he was a man who had seen not a little of the world.

Rigout or Rigord came from Languedoc, and called himself by the proud old name of Goth. Born probably in the neighbourhood of Alais and Uzès, he watched in his youth the terrible excesses of the *chaperons blancs*, and set them down in later years with grim distinctness and sober truth. He became a physician by profession, and at length found a home in the great abbey, where, under the good abbat Hugh Foucaud, he could study to his heart's content. For ten years he was busy with the history of King Philip, even before he was admitted to S. Denys. It was at the urgent request of the abbat that he did not modestly destroy the book when he had written it. The monks knew his powers better than he knew them himself. They set him to write a chronicle of the past kings as well as a record of the deeds of the mighty Philip, and they bade him dedicate to the young Louis the life of his father. In the last decade of the twelfth century and for ten years more he studied as a monk of S. Denys, travelling sometimes abroad, ministering no doubt to the sick in the infirmary, and taking part in the solemn ceremonials with which from time to time the king was received when he came to deposit relics or to redeem vows. Monk, scholar, and physician, he never took upon him the priestly oaths. He gave himself, it would seem, in his later life to the study of Holy Writ and of the lives of the saints, but he knew something too of the old classics. As a historian he was a keen critic, and a severe judge. Though he

dedicated his book to the king's son, and published it
while the king was still on the throne, he was stern in his
condemnation of the cruelty with which Ingeborgis was
treated.   But though he did not hesitate to condemn
the king's crimes, he was among the first to recognise
the vastness of the services which he rendered to France.
It was he who called Philip by the great name of
Augustus, "because he enlarged the boundaries of the
state."   The English chronicles show us that men did
not fear to speak their minds in the thirteenth century,
and Rigord stands forth among the French as a historian
who sought above all things to tell the truth.

But if Philip had his critic among the monks, he
found among the priesthood his most ardent panegyrist.
William, his chaplain, had all the suppleness of a courtier
and much of the genius of a Breton.   Born at some village
on the coast by Finisterre in 1166, he was sent early to
the abbey school of Nantes.   When he was a man he
came to Paris, to study at the University.   He became a
canon of his own diocesan church of Saint Pol de Léon,
and afterwards also of Senlis.   In the prime of life he
entered the court, and Philip at once saw his talents.
From 1200 he was employed again and again in negotiations with the Pope.   Again and again he travelled to
and fro at the king's bidding—"These are not journeys,"
said one who condemned his time-serving; "it is a sojourn that you make at Rome."   To him the king
committed the delicate matter of the divorce proceedings,
and with equal confidence the education of Pierre Charlot,
his bastard son.   When he was not abroad on the king's
business, he was thus constantly at Philip's side.   He
stood by him at the siege of Château Gaillard, and saw

the poor starving folk turned forth by the besieged, on
whom the king had compassion,—and the unhappy man
who still clung to the bone of a dog, and would not give
it up till bread had been put in his mouth. At Dam he
saw the disaster by which the French fleet was burnt.
At Bouvines he stood behind his master, and never far
from him, singing with another clerk the psalm, "Blessed
be the Lord my strength, who teacheth my hands to war,
and my fingers to fight," and "Let God arise," and "The
king shall rejoice in Thy strength, O Lord," as their sobs
and tears allowed. Bouvines was the great day of his
life, and so it seemed to him the centre of all that his
master had done. He set himself to commemorate it in
verse and in prose. The whole of his chronicle served
but as setting for the great triumph, and the *Philippid*
itself is as much a song of Bouvines as an epic of the
life of the king. In later years the writer revised and
reissued the chronicle and the poem which had been the
chief literary work of his life. As a chronicler, he began
by copying and abbreviating Rigord; after 1209 he wrote
chiefly from his personal reminiscences in those events
of which he proudly said, "I have borne a part, and have
seen with my own eyes." He wrote as a frank eulogist;
where Rigord criticised, he suppressed.

The *Philippid*, a laboured but by no means unskilful
poem in twelve books, is a panegyric pure and simple.
It is in form the attempt of a clerical dilletante to adapt
the method of the *Æneid* to the record of the early
thirteenth century; and it is indeed a passable imitation.
The writer has evidently a sense of style and an acquaint-
ance with classic literature which are rare in his day.
But while he believed himself to take his inspiration

from Virgil, he did not scorn to follow also the poets of his own day. Walter of Châtillon in the *Alexandreid* had commemorated the glories of the great Macedonian, Peter Riga had turned Bible history into elegiacs. Philip Augustus was no less valorous than Alexander, and as a defender of the Church he deserved the fame which a zealous churchman could give him in his verse. So said William the Breton when he dedicated his poem to Louis the king's son. The *Philippid* did not go forth to the world with only one patron's name. It invoked the favour also of Pierre Charlot as well as his brothers, for whom also he wrote a *Karolid* which we have lost. In spite of his absurd grandiloquence and the courtier-like embellishments of his record, William the Breton keeps still some of the freshness of a natural and vivacious personality. Personal reminiscence, a memory of childhood or a happy comparison, now and again seem to bring us into the presence of a man who had a kind heart and a keen enjoyment of life,—like the priests of the south in the songs of the Troubadours, he loved the red wine : his poem is full of references to all the wines of his day,—a poet who delighted in his work and magnified his office ; a servant whose loyalty was genuine and came near to hero-worship. The king in the *Philippid*, gigantic though the proportions of his greatness are, never ceases to be a very human character. The little touches of his compassion and his wrath, his tears and his audacity, make him as real to us, if not as lovable, as he was to his enthusiastic chaplain.

The *Philippid*, and the literature of eulogy which it represents, sought to find in the mythical ancestry and the historic succession of the Capetian kings a new

source of romance and dignity. The Franks are descended from Hector, and Philip is the true heir of
Charles the Great, who now with the romancers becomes
Charlemagne, the great hero of legend, the Arthur of a
half-mythical age. The tendency to make the exploits
and character of Charlemagne mythical is a necessary
part of the scheme which makes an epic of King Philip's
life. This imaginative reconstruction of the past was
no doubt far more prominent in the *Karolid* than it is
in the *Philippid*. It went far on the lines of Geoffrey
of Monmouth. It gave to Arthur and his Table Round
a parallel in Charlemagne and his court of peers; and,
just as the Welsh fables had an important bearing on
English politics, so had the French legends a powerful
influence on the construction of the strong monarchy of
Philip Augustus and his successors. King by divine
right and with the sanction to his monarchy of a romantic
and almost illimitable past, Philip appeared before
his court and in the judgment of his contemporaries as
possessed of an indefeasible right to powers which his
feeble predecessor could never exercise. His personal
character supported the claim, and men called him the
"God-given," the "magnanimous," Karolides, Caesar,
and Augustus.

William the Breton was not alone in versifying the
deeds of the great king. Giles of Corbeil, Philip's physician, commemorated his triumphs in a long poem of 5925
hexameters. But his commemoration is only as it were
by accident. He calls his book *Gera Pigra*, and its
main subject is an attack upon the vice and wordliness
of the French clergy. Not the first or the last physician
of the body who did not lie down comfortably with the

physicians of the soul, he exhausts the language of indignant rhetoric to denounce the luxury which he saw around him. As a picture of the social life of the age, his poem, tedious as it is, is valuable, but it does not compare for its direct interest to our subject with the vivacious if voluminous *Philippid*.

As judging Philip from a further distance, Robert of Auxerre, a monk of S. Marianus in that city, whose original contributions to this history of his time extend from 1180 to 1211, supplies a number of facts which other writers have ignored, but he is not an author of the first or second rank.

While in France S. Denys was the great treasure-house of history, and the court the home of romantic legend, both glorifying Philip the Conqueror, foreign historians were little less impressed by his triumphs.

From his early years poets and chroniclers outside his own lands had watched and speculated on his career. "King Philip," says Bertrand de Born, "will he be like his father, or follow the customs of the great Carlo?" "The little king of the great land," the same Troubadour mockingly called him, and he declared that he "has lost his rights because he is so young." But Bertrand, fickle though he was to the Angevin house, was too much of a southern knight to look with any impartial feeling on the northern king. It was different with the chroniclers of Flanders and of England.

Gilbert of Mons, canon of S. Peter at Namur, chancellor of the count Baldwin V. of Hainault, saw French affairs and the character of Philip with a keen but fair vision. He was the chief if not the only statesman who advised the rulers of Hainault in their perilous position between the Empire and the Franks. He was a faithful servant and a true patriot, a man of great parts, a traveller, a diplomatist, just as a statesman and as a historian.   As early as 1184 he had negotiated the grant of the succession of Namur to Baldwin, and in later years was constantly engaged in the intricate discussions and changes which eventually resulted in his master's obtaining that county.   His skill it was that most aided Baldwin VI. in winning Flanders on his uncle's death.   He lived to see the triumph but he did not record the decay of the house of which he was the lifelong servant.   At Mons and at Namur he held ecclesiastical office, and he died, perhaps at S. Germain at Mons, within a few months at most of Philip Augustus himself.   His chronicle of Hainault is a record of facts rather than of judgments, but it deals with facts as they appear to a statesman and a man of affairs.   On King Philip he passes no direct criticism, but while he recognises his power, he does not hesitate to accept as plausible accusations against him of treachery and fraud.   Of the strength and freedom of the Flemish cities, and of the discords to which they led, he gives a vivid picture. But most of all he is a faithful servant of Count Baldwin, "prince most prudent and most powerful, good judge, and very greatly beloved by all his men both small and great."   It is good to read of Philip's acts as they appeared in the eyes of the loyal servitor of his wife's father.

Gilbert of Mons was not alone among those who watched Philip from beyond his northern frontiers. Flemish annalists and historians have many a reference to the growth of his power.   Especially eager was

Tournai and the district round it.   There Philippe
Mouskes, clerk and chronicler, put into popular verse the
alarums and excursions of the daring overlord which he
had witnessed with dismay and amazement.   As close
was the scrutiny of the subjects of the Angevin house.
Robert of Torigny, abbat of S. Michael in peril of the
sea, watched and recorded the beginning of that long
struggle with the young Philip which should give his
beloved Normandy to the Frankish king.

Among many English chroniclers who wrote of
different periods of the long reign of the son of Louis
VII. some need special mention.   Richard Fitz-Neal,
bishop of London, and treasurer of Henry II., was in
possession of information as to all the alliances and the
quarrels between his master and the young Philip; and
Roger of Hoveden, clerk and justice, followed in the
steps of his narration.   Both were men who lived close
to the English kings, and who watched with jealous
interest the rising power of their young French rival.
Rarely do they turn aside from their record of fact,
semi-official as indeed it is, to discuss motives or describe
character, but in brief phrases, as well as in the detailed
account which they give of Philip's movements, they
show the deep interest with which the rise of his power
and the development of his personality were regarded
at the court of the Angevin king.   Less of a courtier,
but as close an observer, was Ralph de Diceto, Dean of
S. Paul's.   He was a personal friend of Richard Fitz-Neal,
bishop, treasurer, and annalist: no less well known was
he to William Longchamp and Walter of Coutances,
the ministers of Richard and of John.   He is especially
full in treating of the life of Philip, not only in his

relations with the English kings, but in his private
affairs, and chiefly his long contest with Innocent III.
on the divorce question. The accuracy of his information, his constant insertion of documents, and his
shrewd judgments, make the work of the Dean of S.
Paul's of great value for the student of Philip's career.

Not only at the centre of public business did English
writers note with surprise and in detail the growth of
the power which rivalled that of their masters.
Monastic chroniclers in the distant country valleys
waited eagerly for information of French doings, and
recorded what they learnt with pious interest. The
Coggeshall chronicler of this period was a writer of no
small ability, and his house had welcomed many a
traveller who could give information at first hand of
the doings of kings and churchmen.   Anselm, King
Richard's chaplain, who was with him in his romantic
adventures after leaving Palestine, Milon, abbat of Pin,
who heard his last confession, themselves told their
experiences to the receptive ear of the Coggeshall
historian, and among their tales the doings of young
Philip were not forgotten.   Thus we find in an English
monastery what is practically a first-hand authority for
some of the chief acts of the French king.

The historian of the priory of Augustinian canons at
Newburgh, living far indeed from the great events he
described, gives some of the most valuable information
which we possess as to the last years of Henry II., the
reign of Richard I., and the steady growth of the
strength of the Frankish monarchy. He dwells with
persistent iteration on the bitter jealousy which Philip
showed during the Crusade, on the " venomous workings

of his mind," his "evil eye and galled imagination," his eagerness to defame Richard's character. Of Philip's personal history William of Newburgh was as intimately informed. He passed a severe judgment on his conduct towards Ingeborgis, and no less on the "execrable perjury of two false bishops," the bishop of Beauvais and the bishop of Chartres, who pronounced the divorce. Yet Philip is to him still "noble" and "most illustrious," and the French king has, it is clear, not a little of the Englishman's sympathy in his endeavours to win for himself the lands of the Angevins. William of Newburgh died probably in 1198, so that we have nothing from his hand of the triumphs of King Philip.

A greater historian than these, Matthew Paris, the chronicler of S. Alban's, was a diplomatist as well as a monk, and he had considerable knowledge of public affairs. But as he was probably not born before 1195, his information becomes of primary value only at the period when Philip had won Normandy and was about to triumph over the great coalition of his foes. Here he makes most important additions to our knowledge. We derive from him better than from any other writer a vivid impression of the English feeling which did so much to render Philip's success possible, and to which it was not altogether unwelcome. For the stormy days of Louis's invasion there is no authority more valuable than Matthew Paris.

It is not surprising that the clerks who saw the working out of those vices which brought about the fall of the Angevins, should turn for contrast to the French court. In few of the English writers is there much bitter feeling against the French monarchs : but in one, a Welshman and one who claimed to be littèrateur as well as historian, there is an approach to deliberate and exaggerated eulogy of Philip the Conqueror. Gerald de Barri, archdeacon of S. David's, had long experience of the Angevins' treachery and ingratitude. Henry II. he regarded as an incarnation of the vilest vices, and his sons as born to cause the destruction of their house. When he wrote his curious treatise on the "Instruction of Princes," a book which he kept by him till old age to alter and revise, he lost no chance of praising Louis VII. and his son at the expense of their rivals. When he issued his final version of the work, on which he had bestowed so much pains, he would dedicate it, he said, if to any one, to Louis of France, King Philip's son, because he was from his tenderest years a friend to letters, and because, it is clear, he regarded the failure of his English expedition with the bitterest regret. Giraldus watched the career of the great Philip with the keenest interest. From his cradle he records the visions of his fame, and he preserves little stories of the sayings and adventures of his boyhood, which show something of a personal affection and admiration for the gallant king. Most clearly of all does he show in what direction his sympathies flow by a comparison of the French with the English court—a comparison of peculiar interest.

"At this point," he says, after speaking of the modest claim of Louis VII. for his beautiful realm, the land of chivalry and valour, that it had "bread and wine and pleasure"; "at this point, this seems meet to be added, that in the court of the kings of France no one sees

anything of mere show or of tyranny. They do not
load themselves with warlike weapons in time of peace.
An object of loathing to none of their subjects, they
deserve to be an object of affection to all, seeing that
they do not employ rods or sticks, chamberlains or
attendants, to debar individuals with grievances from
access to their person. At the court of France justice
is ever at hand; it is prompt and free, not put up for
sale, nor made the object of that vile and accursed
traffic and sin of simony. Nor, as elsewhere, is justice,
an attribute so priceless and divine, con-substantial and
co-eternal with God Himself, prostituted in that shameful way, by being invariably put off from day to day
with the harshness of caprice.

"Again, the rulers of other lands throughout their
conversation make use of strange oaths, such as 'od's
death, or eyes, or feet, or teeth, or throat, venturing on
oaths as foolish as they are indiscriminate. While they
show their hardihood in thus tearing the Deity limb
from limb, they also show that they neither fear nor
revere the excellence of the Divine majesty with that
devotion which is its due. The kings of France, on the
other hand, whenever they think fit to make use of
oaths in their speech, swear by the saints of France
either under their simple names, or with the addition of
their titles, with the view of filling out and embellish-
ing their conversation. And it is not in words alone,
but in almost every act that they aim at simplicity,
knowing as they do that 'he who walketh simply,
walketh surely.'

"Again, they do not behave as bears or lions in the
presence of their subjects, as we have seen some rulers

do. Nay, though they are exalted on the earth, they
display affability and kindness towards their inferiors ;
instead of being insolent and haughty, they are the
rather lowly and courteous. They know and remember
that they are but men, and recall the saying of the wise
man 'they have made thee a ruler ; be not elated, but
be among thy subjects as one who is of them,' and that
other saying 'if thou art great, humble thyself in all
things.'

" Again, many a ruler have we seen who, when in the
chances of war or the hazards of fortune he has
achieved some praiseworthy success, immediately in the
excess of his pride ascribes it entirely to his own right
hand. But the kings of France in every success bestow
praise on the exceeding great mercy and power of
Heaven, and to God alone give all the thanks and
glory, whenever they have performed some action which
has brought them thanks or earned them glory.

" There have been rulers too, aye, and are in our days,
who treat justice and injustice as universally equivalent,
who absolutely ignore the distinctions of right and
wrong, who, regarding their will as law, neither secure
justice to their subjects, nor preserve inviolate the troth
and honour of the marriage tie. With unpardonable
effrontery they disobey the dictates of honour and
justice in the full light of day, setting by their sinful
conduct an unholy precedent for sin. In the case of
the kings of France, however, a sense of purity and
honour, deserving of all praise in a ruler, preserves
unsullied the sanctity of the lawful bond ; while the
impartiality of the scales of justice, and the fairness of
the methods of government, like precious jewels brought

from every quarter, shed a becoming lustre on the throne of the ruling sovereign.

" Again, I have seen rulers who, instead of succeeding to the crown in turn according to lineal descent, prefer to put the cart before the horse, and by means of the wholesale slaughter of their kinsmen to secure for themselves a sovereignty of violence. For their excesses of bloodshed, tyranny, and cruelty they experience even in this world the retribution of divine vengeance. By arrows and crossbolts, in many a war-like encounter and many a hostile inroad, they die unnatural deaths, and await in another world the ever-lasting punishment of the torments of Gehenna. Neither to their sons nor grandsons, nor yet to any other relation, do they bequeath what they have won by foul means, and held by fouler; their rule is throughout marked by unprincipled transgressions. The kings of France, on the other hand, invariably attain to their father's realm by the natural right of hereditary succession; they are in the highest degree moderate, respectful, and lenient towards their subjects; they avoid cruelty and outrage in their government. There-fore it is, that in their long reigns of undisturbed prosperity, God, Who even in this world sometimes bestows some recognition on good deserts, grants them from day to day increase of honour in ever fuller measure, and when at length the course of this temporal life is run, they die a blessed death, and handing on to their sons and heirs their realms in happy succession, they receive in heaven the everlasting reward of their own godly and righteous government.

" Again, some rulers, as a sign of high spirit, have a

preference for savage and ravening beasts, such as bears,
leopards, lions, to be carried before them, painted on
armour or (embroidered on) standards : they are
desirous apparently of being likened to these creatures
among their fellow-men. The kings of France, alone,
set a praiseworthy example ; not only in word and
gesture, but in their every act their one desire is to
attain moderation and humility, to avoid arrogance and
haughtiness. Thus it is that they mark and adorn
their shields, standards, and the rest of their armour
with nothing but the simple flowerets of the fleur-de-lys.
It is strange, and as deserving of honourable record as
it is worthy of all praise, that in these days of ours (to
anticipate a little), we have seen these simple flowers
overcome the pards and lions. These awe-inspiring
beasts—so marvellous are the turns of fortune—at the
first breath of these Frankish flowers turned to instant
and craven flight. Without a glance behind, without
another struggle, they abandoned, among the very first-
fruits of the war, all their caves and dens, all their
wonted haunts and lairs, together with spoil untold,
pastures rich and wide and studded with flowers. Then
was fulfilled, as in many other cases, the gospel sentence
pronounced by the infallible lips of Truth itself, 'He
that humbleth himself shall be exalted, and he that
exalteth himself shall be abased.'

" Again, in these latter days of ours, there have been
rulers who, as if war had been declared, have constantly
laid grasping and plundering hands on God's property.
They have not permitted the bride of Christ, which He
purchased for Himself, and for whose welfare He shed
His blood, to enjoy any freedom in their realms.

Therefore has Heaven made of them all an awful example, and brought upon them the exquisite retribution they deserved. Their own children, brought up in evil ways, have risen up in arms against their fathers from their very boyhood, and harassed them with constant and effective persecution. From the very realms in which these rulers forbade the worship of God with due rights, Heaven has granted that powerful avengers of the flourishing stock of Pepin and Charles should spring, to take up the cause of vengeance and drive them forth root and branch in sorrow and disgrace. For their evil deeds they have been irrevocably driven forth, not only from this world of the dying, but from that other world of the living; not only from this world of punishment and death, but from that other world of life; not only from this world which we tread, but from that other world which we seek. Would to Heaven that they had not brought this fate upon their heads! But the kings of France in their realms zealously render unto God the things which are God's, leaving to the prelates, untouched and unimpaired, the right of handling and dispensing ecclesiastical law, together with all their dignities and liberties. In this, as in other spheres, they receive their reward. For a rule so righteous and godly they earn for themselves on earth great increase of honour, and in heaven, after the course of this temporal life, the imperishable meed of a triumphal crown.

"Deservedly, then, and by the manifest sentence of the heavenly Judge, is it that the realms of tyrants so utterly wicked and perverted as those whom I have mentioned and noted above, through a divine dispensation, which even in this world sometimes rewards the good and evil according to their deserts, have now by force of arms passed into the possession of godly and kindly rulers, deserving of praise in every quarter of the globe —the rulers whose character and habits I have partially sketched. The course of events would doubtless have been the same in England as in the realm of the Franks if England had shown to the Church that faith and loyalty, that accord and respect which are her due. But of this enough."

Whatever allowance may be made for the wounded vanity of Giraldus at the persistent ignoring of his claims to high office, which had been the studied policy of Henry II., Richard I., and John, it is clear enough that such an eulogy of the French royal house, however exaggerated, must have had some real foundation in a dignity and grandeur which impressed contemporaries. For the reason of this impression we have not far to seek. Philip was the centre of a court which was the resort of great soldiers, great lawyers, and great priests. The poem of William the Breton shows us how close Philip lived to the *familiares* of his household. Guèrin the Hospitaller, the bishop-elect of Senlis, who fought so manfully and planned with such skill on the great day of Bouvines, was much more than a minister of the king, he was his dear friend. The language of Giraldus indeed suggests that the French kings lived in more amiable fashion with their men than did the "demon race" of the Angevins. Guèrin certainly was in the most critical period of the reign always at the king's right hand. Philip would listen to him, even in the delicate matter of Ingeborgis, when he would hear no one else.

The clerks who sate in the council, the lawyers and diplomatists who carried out his policy, formed a close circle round the king.　And beside them were the young barons of the *maison du roi*, the men who saved his life at Bouvines, and whom charter after charter rewards with lands and privileges.　But to the outside world the court of the great Capetian king remained ever more or less of a mystery.　The fact that for a long time there was no queen to dispense courteşies and to attract maidens and their lovers to her side, in itself set a gulf between court and people. Men knew that their lord did not live an austere life, and yet he could hardly ever be called a popular king. There were days, as on his return from his great victory over the three allied Powers, and when he took his ill-used wife again to his side, when his people's hearts seemed to go out to him.　But on the whole he lived a solitary and unsympathetic life.　A great king, cease-lessly active, of unwearied vigilance and ever-changing scheme, he was stern, secret, subtle, obstinate, and invincibly patient in the pursuit of what his eye desired and his hand found to do.　And this character im-pressed itself year by year more clearly on the men of his age, so that as the days went on they became more reticent in writing of him, and the burst of spring-tide enthusiasm which hailed his accession died down at the end of his life into the most meagre record of his acts.　The astute sovereign who began life so gallantly had become more and more of a grim enigma to his subjects.　They had woven legends about his life.　He had become a Charlemagne, the mysterious, half-magical sovereign, rather than a gallant knight-errant of poesy;

and each romance took his real personality farther from his people's sight. New men arose who carried on his work without any of his own characteristics. The hot-headed, gallant Louis—ever ready to break a lance or lead a forlorn hope—began with his pious, domineering, Spanish wife, to fill a space in the popular eye from which the great conqueror had receded. Still the old king lived on, silent and self-contained, deep in schemes and very chary of action. He would not lift his hand to a romantic enterprise outside his own land. He watched and waited for results which he foresaw.

And so death came to him as he quietly continued the work of consolidation and order on which he had set his heart. He passed from district to district hearing complaints, redressing wrongs, rewarding faithful service. He bent his mind to knit the newly won provinces to the central power. Privileges overflowed to the towns of Normandy, Anjou, and Touraine. New barons were given new fiefs. And over all the king watched closely, but with patience. Augustus he was called, said Rigord, because of the vast additions he had made to the royal domain. Since his accession Vermandois, Poitou, Anjou, Touraine, Maine, Alençon, Clermont in Beauvaisis, Beaumont, Ponthieu, Artois, Amiens, Valois, and, greatest of all, the duchy of Normandy, had been added to the territory of the French crown. By purchase, by exchange, by treaty of alliance, a heritage almost as great had come into the king's hands. He might well feel that his work was done.

Philip had lived a hard life. He had been on crusade. He had not spared himself in marches or in vigils by the camp-fire. At home he had been no more prudent than the other monarchs of his day. At fifty-eight he was already an old man. He had a son of thirty-six who had won his spurs in England and in the South. In the autumn of 1222 he began to suffer from a wasting fever, but still he worked as before. He was spared his father's sad end of impotence and decay. At Pacy, in July 1223, he had summoned a council to provide against one of the small baronial outbreaks which even the persistent vigilance of his long reign had not entirely suppressed. He felt himself sickening and gave himself into the hands of his physicians. Yet he seemed for several days to rally. He determined to go home to his new tower, the Louvre. On Tuesday, July 11, he had felt better. On Wednesday he was worse, and received the last sacraments. But he still kept on his journey to Mantes. There on Thursday he rested, and on Friday the 14th he passed away.

So died Philip the illustrious king of the Franks, writes the chronicler of S. Denys, "a man of high prudence by nature and by art, mighty in valour, glorious in his deeds, renowned in fame, victorious in battles, who wondrously enlarged the rights and the power of the realm of the Franks and enriched the royal treasure; for against many renowned princes, powerful in their lands, their arms and their wealth, did he manfully contend, and conquered. A mighty defender and protector was he also of the churches, and specially the holy church of S. Denys did he, with peculiar favour and with, as it were, a largess of love, nourish and guard, and prove by many an effectual deed the fondness which he had towards it. Zealous from his early years for the Christian faith, in his youth he affixed the cross to his breast and warred over sea against the Saracens with a strong hand. And moreover when verging on old age he spared not his own son, but sent him twice against the heretic Albigenses with great cost and expense, and both in life and in death spent largely himself in that business. Above all things he was most generous in giving to the poor and spreading charity in many a place." They made for the great king a great burying. S. Denys received him with all its dignity and pomp. The archbishops of Rheims and Sens were there, and twenty bishops, among them the pope's legate, Conrad, bishop of Porto, and Pandulf, bishop of Norwich, and the faithful Guèrin, bishop of Senlis, the right hand of the dead king. At the same time at two altars the requiem mass was said by the pope's legate and William of Joinville, archbishop of Rheims. The tears coursed down Louis's cheeks, says William the Breton, as he followed his father's body to the tomb. By him stood his half-brother, Philip Hurepel, the legitimated offspring of the unhappy union with Agnes of Meran, and John of Brienne, king of Jerusalem.

There was no doubt or danger as to the succession. Louis had long been in possession of a separate provision and a considerable power. Married in 1200 to Blanche of Castile, niece of King John, he had received Issoudun, Graçay, and large fiefs in Berry, as his wife's dowry, and nine years later he had been given by his father great estates in the South. Vermandois and Artois were practically recognised as his property, and as count of Artois he treated separately with the Flanders in 1212.

He had long been employed by the king in important diplomatic missions, and his expeditions to England, to Poitou, and to Toulouse, had shown him possessed of the spirit and energy which the great conqueror looked for in his heir. All men spoke well of him as a Christian knight and a man of honour. At his side was an intrepid and capable woman, worthy to share his throne, and, it was already evident, to guide his counsels. His eldest living son was already nine years old. The monarchy of Philip Augustus was too strong to need the support of a coronation of the heir. The constantly repeated election for the benefit of the same family had become merely a formal recognition of the right of hereditary succession. Louis was the first of his house who was not crowned in the lifetime of his predecessor. The force of routine and the strength of Philip Augustus had firmly established the doctrine of hereditary right.

The two children of Agnes of Meran had already been provided for. Within a year of the birth of Philip Hurepel, and before he had been recognised as legitimate, treaties had been drawn up to establish his position. He had been married when he was nine years old and knighted in 1222. He was fixed in the position of a baron of the second rank. His sister Mary had been betrothed in 1202 to Arthur of Brittany. Four years later she was betrothed to Philip of Namur, whom she married in 1210. On his death she married Henry of Brabant, but the marriage failed to secure her father against her husband's hostility in 1214.

Philip had left a will, written in the September of 1222, when he felt his sickness coming upon him. He left

behind him an enormous treasure, which proved his careful management and his skilful treatment of the royal
domain.   He directed that a large sum should be distributed among those from whom he had unjustly extorted.
A hundred and fifty thousand marks of silver he left,
for the succour of the Holy Land, to the Templars and
Hospitallers, and to John of Brienne.   His jewels he left
to the monks of S. Denys.   They were bought back by
his successor, leaving only a golden cross which the
abbey retained.   To his long-suffering wife Ingeborgis
and others, and to the poor, he left legacies, and interpret-
ing his wishes some money was given to Amaury de
Montfort after his death.   The will, in strict feudal
fashion, concerns only the treasury.   The royal domain
is left untouched.   Philip's grandfather, Louis VI., had
begun the wise policy of leaving to his younger children
only the position of vassals of the second rank.   His
example was followed by the Conqueror.   He left to
his son, Philip Hurepel, only the county of Clermont in
the Beauvaisis, which he had acquired on the extinction
of the male line of the house of Chartres.   He had
already been invested with the county of Boulogne,
forfeited by the traitor Reginald whose daughter he
had married.

Philip, unlike many of his fathers, left no legacy of
difficulties and disunion for his heir.   Of the forty-three
years of his reign at least twenty-six had been years of
war, and from each war the monarchy had risen stronger
than before.   To restore his power to the strength of
that of Charles the Great, men said he had declared to
be his aim.   He had done as much as one man could do
to accomplish the task.   He had found France a small

realm hedged in by mighty rivals. When he began to
reign, but a very small portion of the French-speaking
people had owned his sway. As suzerain his power
was derided. Even as immediate lord he was defied
and set at nought. But when he died the whole face
of France was changed. The king of the Franks was
undisputedly the king of by far the greater part of the
land. And the internal strength of his government
had advanced as rapidly and as securely as the external
power. Philip Augustus was the first of his race who
could reign if he willed as a despot. In conquering
the Angevins he had succeeded to something of the
characteristics of their government. The master of
Rouen and of Angers was a different man from the mere
lord of Paris and Orleans.

The march of the monarchy under Philip the Conqueror by changing the face of France changed the
history of Europe. It placed a new power among the
great states, which should henceforth exercise a commanding influence. It had been Philip's task to found
France in the sense in which we now use the word.
Under him the king of the Franks is first clearly seen
to be sovereign of Gaul. Great as a conqueror, he was
even greater in constructive and unifying power. What
he found he consolidated, and what he founded he laid
firm. In a century of great men, beside Innocent III.
and Frederic I. and Henry II. and S. Bernard, he
stands with the greatest. In his work and in himself
he is worthy to take place among the great statesmen
who have made the Europe of to-day.

NOTE

In writing this book I have found the conclusions which I had drawn from the original authorities so constantly anticipated by the French and German historians who have studied the subject within the last fifty years, that I have often had no other course open to me but to follow closely in the path that they had marked out. The plan of this series does not allow me to mention my obligations as they occur. I have only, therefore, to say that I am very greatly indebted to the works of MM. Luchaire (*Institutions Monarchiques*, and *Communes françaises*), Léopold Delisle (*Catalogue des actes de Philippe Auguste*), Davidsohn (*Philip August und Ingeborg*), W. Walker (*Increase of Royal Power under Philip Augustus*), and to many articles in the *Revue Historique*, and *Revue des Questions Historiques*, by MM. Castellieri, Lot, and others, as well as to older works, such as Hurter's *Innocent III.*, and books on points of military history, etc. I have named the chief chroniclers in my last chapter, but I cannot forbear to express my admiration of the admirable edition of *Rigord* and *William the Breton* which we owe to the labour of M. Delaborde. My book, if nothing else, should be a tribute of homage to the French historians, my masters.

W. H. H.